Learning from the BRICS

LEARNING FROM THE BRICS
OPEN ACCESS TO SCIENTIFIC INFORMATION IN EMERGING COUNTRIES

Edited by
JOACHIM SCHÖPFEL

Departement of Information and Document Sciences,
University of Lille (France)

Litwin Books
Sacramento, CA

Copyright 2015 respective authors.

Published in 2015 by Litwin Books

Litwin Books, LLC
PO Box 188784
Sacramento, CA 95818

http://litwinbooks.com

This book is printed on acid-free, sustainably-sourced paper.

Library of Congress Cataloging-in-Publication Data

Learning from the BRICS : open access to scientific information in emerging countries / edited by Joachim Schöpfel, Departement of Information and Document Sciences, University of Lille (France).
    pages cm
    Includes bibliographical references and index.
    ISBN 978-1-936117-84-0 (alk. paper)
    1. Science publishing--BRIC countries. 2. Technical publishing--BRIC countries. I. Schöpfel, Joachim, 1957-
    Z286.S4L43 2015
    070.5'7--dc23
                                2015006744

Table of Contents

Preface 1
Introduction: Open Access to Scientific Information
in Emerging Countries 7
    Open science… 7
    … and open access 8
    From global thinking… 10
    …to local action 12
    Learning from emerging countries 13
    Overview 15
    References 18

Facts & Figures: Brazil 21
    Country and Economy 21
    Research and Open Access 22
    Overview 23
    About the Author 25

The SciELO Program and Gold Road Open Access 27
    Introduction 27
    The origins and consolidation of gold road OA in the Latin
    American and Caribbean region 29
    The development of the SciELO model 38

The journals in the SciELO Network–the case of Brazil 46
The way forward–priority action lines 50
Conclusion 55
Bibliographic References 58

FACTS & FIGURES: RUSSIAN FEDERATION 61
Country and Economy 61
Research and Open Access 62
Overview 63
About the Authors 65

OPEN ACCESS IN RUSSIA: THE BEGINNING OF A LONG WAY 67
Back in the USSR 67
Empirical elements 69
The heritage of history: from grey literature to open access 70
OA to published information sources 75
Legal aspects 83
Concluding remarks 86
References 89

FACTS & FIGURES: INDIA 91
Country and Economy 91
Research and Open Access 92
Overview 93
About the Author 95

OPEN ACCESS IN INDIA: AWARENESS AND ACCEPTANCE OF
INSTITUTIONAL REPOSITORIES AND OPEN ACCESS JOURNALS 97
Introduction 97
The penetration of the Open Access concept in India 98
Institutional repositories 99
Research studies on Indian institutional repositories 102
Open Access journals: India a leader at global front 104
Studies related to attitudes of Indian authors towards
Open Access journals 106
The dark side of Open Access journal publishing 108

Current updates on Open Access movement in India (May 2014) 110
Capacity building & Open Access curriculum for researchers and library and information professionals: Indian initiatives 113
Perspectives 113
Acknowledgement 116
References 117

FACTS & FIGURES: CHINA 123
Country and Economy 123
Research and Open Access 124
Overview 125
About the Author 127

OPEN ACCESS IN CHINA: THE DEVELOPMENT OF OPEN ACCESS JOURNALS 129
Introduction 129
Literature review 130
Methodology 132
Results and discussion 133
Summary 144
Eight strategies for OA journal development 147
References 150

FACTS & FIGURES: SOUTH AFRICA 153
Country and Economy 153
Research and Open Access 154
Overview 155
About the Authors 157

SOUTH AFRICA: THE ROLE OF OPEN ACCESS IN PROMOTING LOCAL CONTENT, INCREASING ITS USAGE AND IMPACT AND PROTECTING IT 159
Introduction 159
Open Access and the African philosophy of "Ubuntu" 160
Open access, basic human rights and social justice 161
The South African research landscape and open access 164

vii

- Institutional repositories 165
- Significance of promoting access 166
- From brain drain to brain gain: the role of open access 167
- Impact 169
- Paradox in open access 170
- Protection and preservation of local content 171
- South African government institutions and support for open access 174
- Librarians, scientists and publishers 176
- Survey of the South African open access landscape 177
- Summary and conclusion 185
- References 187

CONCLUSION: ROUNDTABLE 191
- Key factors for success 192
- Challenges 193
- Green v gold road to open access 195
- The public sector 195
- Cooperation 196
- An alternative model? 198
- Learning from the BRICS 199

FURTHER READING 201
WEB RESOURCES 203
- Declarations 203
- Directories 203
- News, blogs, other sites 204

INDEX 206

PREFACE
Michael Jubb

The drivers behind the open access movement are clear and strong. The internet has already enhanced and accelerated the flows of information and knowledge created by researchers. But so much more could be achieved if the barriers inherent in the business models that have underpinned scholarly publishing over 350 years were to be removed. Worldwide open access could help to achieve a number of goals. First, it could improve the efficiency of the research process itself, by increasing the volume of information that is readily accessible to researchers, reducing the time taken to find and access it, and facilitating the use of up-to-date tools to organise, manipulate and analyse it. Second, it could promote greater engagement between the professional research community and those sections of the general public who have an interest in the results of research, and thus bring greater transparency, openness and accountability. Third, it could help to overcome the gaps that sometimes get in the way of relationships and linkages between basic and applied research on the one hand, and the people and organisations who have an interest in making use of new knowledge to achieve innovations in the form of new products and services, thus enhancing public welfare and economic growth. Fourth, it could in all these ways improve the social and economic returns on the substantial investments made in research, especially those made by Governments and by the many bodies in the voluntary sector which fund research.

The last decade and a half has seen a growing recognition and acknowledgement on the part of researchers, universities and research institutions, funders and governments across the world of the ways in which open access could help to achieve all these highly-desirable goals. And the movement is indeed global in reach. The past three years have seen significant policy initiatives from major research nations including the Office of Science and Technology Policy in the USA[1]: the National Natural Science Foundation of China (NSFC) and the Chinese Academy of Sciences (CAS); and the Higher Education Funding Councils[2] and Research Councils UK (RCUK)[3]. International bodies have been active too: the recent statement on the principles of open access to the scientific record endorsed by the General Assembly of the International Council for Science (ICSU) in September 2014[4] was preceded by an Action Plan towards Open Access[5] issued by the Global Research Council in 2013. And as this set of essays makes clear, there have been significant developments in the BRICS countries.

Progress has of course been slower than many open access advocates had hoped in the heady days between 2000 and 2003 when the Budapest, Bethesda and Berlin Declarations were being drafted and promulgated, and new open access publishers such as BioMed Central and PLoS were being established. The shift from print to almost-wholly online provision and access to scholarly journals–which was in retrospect achieved relatively quickly–proved much less problematic than overturning, through a wholesale and global shift to open access, a basic publishing business model that has been established and nourished for 350 years. If we knew how to overcome all the barriers, we surely should have done so by now.

---

1   http://www.whitehouse.gov/sites/default/files/microsites/ostp/ostp_public_access_memo_2013.pdf,

2   http://www.hefce.ac.uk/whatwedo/rsrch/rinfrastruct/oa/policy/

3   http://www.rcuk.ac.uk/research/openaccess/policy/

4   http://www.icsu.org/general-assembly/news/ICSU%20Report%20on%20Open%20Access.pdf

5   http://www.globalresearchcouncil.org/sites/default/files/pdfs/grc_action_plan_open_access%20FINAL.pdf

Perhaps the biggest barrier is that moving to open access requires action from a number of different parties in the ecosystem of scholarly communications. Policy-makers at national and international levels, along with funding organisations and individual universities and research institutions, can set conditions and exert considerable influence. But the great majority of them have been reluctant to move from facilitating and promoting open access to establishing and effectively enforcing a requirement that all research should be published on open access terms. Hence there has often been a gap between policy aspiration and implementation at scale.

Practical support for implementation has been largely the responsibility of two kinds of organisations with very different perspectives and interests. On the one hand, funding bodies and universities have taken on the task of providing funds to support open access – whether that be in the form of money to meet the costs of article processing/publishing charges (APCs) or to set up repositories – and to develop a sustainable open access infrastructure. On the other hand, publishers – both the established ones and many new entrants to the market – have responded to the new environment and to policy initiatives by establishing new open access journals, translating established journals into open access mode, or at the least shifting journals to the hybrid model or modifying their policies in relation to deposit and access via repositories. The global picture at all these levels is mixed, and it is still changing.

But individual researchers and research teams still play a dominant role in determining the speed of progress towards open access. They clearly have a major influence on policy-making by funders, universities and other research institutions, as well as on publishers. And so long as policy mandates remain loose, or are not rigorously enforced, researchers' decisions on the journals to which they submit their articles are one of the key determinants of progress. Evidence from reports and surveys over many years indicates that researchers' awareness of and attitudes towards open access have grown positively and steadily over recent years. The evidence also suggests that both the increasing availability of open access options and the development and implementation of policy initiatives from funders and research institutions have a positive effect on researchers, their perceptions and their propensity to adopt open access. But most researchers – as well as the institutions in which they work–operate in a highly-competitive environment; and it is still the case that in most of the leading research nations in Europe and North America, researchers' choice of the journals in which to publish their work tends to be dominated by their perceptions of the quality of those journals, and the credit they will gain by publishing in them. For most researchers, open access tends to be a secondary consideration. There are some signs that this may be changing – see, for example, the shifts in attitudes shown in the latest in a series of survey reports from the publishers Taylor and Francis[6]–but there is still clearly some way to go.

In this context, it is of particular interest to note in the contributions to this collection of essays a repeated emphasis on quality, and the drive to enhance the international standing as well as the impact and the local influence of the research communities in the BRICS countries. Those communities have over the past decade grown in size, productivity and influence much faster than their colleagues in the more-well-established research nations, and that trend will surely continue for the foreseeable future. It is also clear that the performance of BRICS researchers is under-recorded in many of the standard measures established and developed to record and assess the performance of the research communities in the global north, and that is well-documented in the essays in this volume. The steps being taken in Brazil and Latin America, and more broadly, to remedy that deficiency are most welcome; and promoting as well as facilitating open access in practical ways will be an important part of that. As a number of the essays make clear, however, the challenges to be met in the transition to open access are as powerful in the BRICS as they are in the global north. Meeting and overcoming them requires concerted and determined action from governments, funding organisations, universities and, not least, researchers themselves.

---

6   http://www.tandfonline.com/page/openaccess/opensurvey/2014

ABOUT THE AUTHOR

Michael Jubb has more than twenty-five years' experience in research policy, funding and administration, as well as scholarly communications. He has served as Deputy Secretary of the British Academy and Deputy Chief Executive of the Arts and Humanities Research Board, overseeing its transition to Research Council status in 2005. He is the founding Director of the Research Information Network, where he has worked with a range of organisations with a stake in scholarly communications, on issues ranging from researchers' use of library and information services, to the economics of scholarly communications. He was Secretary to the Finch Committee in 2011-13, and was responsible for the drafting both of its original report (2012) and the subsequent report (2013) on progress in the implementation of its recommendations.

Introduction: Open Access to Scientific Information in Emerging Countries
Joachim Schöpfel

Open science...

The village of mankind is faced with global challenges. Health, transport, energy, food, climate, security, education and innovation are issues that transcend national boundaries and cannot be resolved by any one country acting alone.

Science is expected to produce helpful knowledge and to contribute to the sustainable development of open society and humanity. Yet, a better understanding of society, nature and environment requires open science, free debate of ideas and exchange of procedures and results. Discussion, readiness to learn from each other and rational criticism are conditions for scientific progress.

Three hundred years ago, in the Age of Enlightenment, European and North-American intellectuals proclaimed themselves as the "Republic of Letters", an open community of scholars, writers and philosophers corresponding through letters, papers and pamphlets on new ideas, observations and experiences. Their free floating conversation at distance, between the salons, societies and academies in London, Paris, Amsterdam and Philadelphia, created the crucial environment for the development of modern scientific research and teaching, against obscurantism and ignorance.

Yesterday, in the Gutenberg era, openness and freedom of discussion was guaranteed by public correspondence and the invention of academic journals, such as the French *Journal des Sçavans* or the *Philosophical Transactions* published by the Royal Society in London. The digital revolution created a knowledge-based society ruled by new information and communication technologies, infrastructures and media. Internet changed research, collaboration and academic publishing. Today, in the galaxy of Internet and virtual networks, openness of scientific communication calls for other solutions.

In the emerging information age, some people consider knowledge as a strategic weapon, as an argument in global competition. Knowledge is more than that. It is a cultural heritage and a common good, produced by society and indispensable for progress and development. Benjamin Franklin once said, "An investment in knowledge pays the best interest". Investment in knowledge means learning and also teaching, thinking and also talking, producing and also communicating. Knowledge must be shared to make sense and be useful. The best interest of knowledge in the beginning of the 21st century is sustainable development and survival. More than ever open society needs open science, a second scientific revolution (Bartling & Friesike 2014) where scientists share their results straight away and with a wide audience.

... AND OPEN ACCESS

Access to information plays a critical role in supporting development[1]. Open access to scientific information is one solution. The basic idea is simple: "Make research literature available online without price barriers and without most permission barriers" (Suber 2012, p.8). Free availability on the public internet and in particular on the easily accessible World Wide Web, includes the permission "for any users to read, download, copy, distribute, print, search, or link to the full texts of these articles, crawl them for indexing, pass them as data to software, or use them for any other lawful purpose, without financial,

---

1   See IFLA's Lyon declaration launched at the 2014 World Library and Information Congress.

legal, or technical barriers other than those inseparable from gaining access to the internet itself" (Budapest Declaration).

In 1999 a meeting in Santa Fe, New Mexico, laid the technical foundation for open access, i.e. the Open Archives Initiative (OAI) and the OAI Protocol for Metadata Harvesting (OAI-PMH). The objective was to create a global open access community, to raise awareness on open access to scientific information and to foster the development of interoperable open access platforms and infrastructures compliant with the OAI protocol. "Hopes were high", remembers Eric F. Van de Velde, technology consultant and former computer scientist at Caltech, "hopes for universal free access to scientific literature, for open access journals, lower-priced journals, access to data, and for better research infrastructures". Half a generation later, the success of open access cannot be denied. And even if not all high hopes have come true, "none of the unfulfilled dreams can detract from the many significant accomplishments of the Open Access Movement"[2].

The first international open repository "arXiv" was launched in 1991 by the High Physics community in Los Alamos. The site invited scientists to deposit their papers at the same time as when they submit them to journals. The objective was direct scientific communication, making papers available to the whole community immediately, often several months before formal publishing.

With nearly one million items, arXiv is still one of the most successful models of the so-called "green road" to open access. "Green road" means self-archiving, i.e. the practice of depositing one's own work in an open repository. The Directory of Open Access Repositories OpenDOAR contains more than 2,700 open repositories but the real number is certainly higher. Most of them are run by universities, faculties, departments, laboratories or other research institutions, for instance by the MIT, Columbia University or Harvard, while others are disciplinary, cross-institutional subject repositories. Open repositories cover all disciplines, and they contain all document types, mostly articles but also theses and dissertations, reports, conference proceedings, unpublished working papers etc. More recently, some institutions launched so-called data repositories, for the deposit and free dissemination of all kinds of research results, raw data and so on.

---

2 Eric Van de Velde on his blog http://scitechsociety.blogspot.com/

Along with open repositories, research communities and the publishing industry developed another mode of open access, the so-called "gold road" which means open access delivered by journals. The Directory of Open Access Journals (DOAJ) lists about 10,000 journals that do not charge readers or their institutions for access and that assign the right of users to "read, download, copy, distribute, print, search, or link to the full texts of these articles", that exercise peer-review or editorial quality control and that report primary results of research or overviews of research results to a scholarly community.

Most of them are funded by subsidies from research organizations, governments or learned societies while about 30% charge Article Processing Charges (APC) in order to cover publishing costs and generate revenues. APC means that authors or their institutions have to pay a publication fee for each accepted paper that may range from less than hundred to four thousand US dollars or more.

Nobody can say exactly how many scientific papers are available in open access and which part of all scientific output they represent. The Bielefeld Academic Search Engine indexes nearly 65 million scientific open access web resources[3]. A recent study on open access claims a percentage of 50% articles even if 20% seems more realistic. What is sure is that this figure differs among disciplines and varies because of institutional decisions, national policies and infrastructures. In some scientific fields such as physics and mathematics, open access has more success than in humanities or chemistry. Some institutions decided on a mandatory approach that commits their scientists to deposit publications in institutional repositories. In the same way, some governments and funding bodies invested in open access infrastructures and/or decided to link research funding to open access dissemination of results, to facilitate uptake and accelerate the transition to open science.

FROM GLOBAL THINKING...

Open access to scientific information and research data is a global concept, with a universal approach to human knowledge and society. "How knowledge circulates", stated John Willinsky from the MIT, "has always been vital to the life of the mind (and) to the well-being of humanity" (2012, p.207). This "access principle" was developed to solve some concrete problems, like the serials crisis, restricted access

---

3   http://www.base-search.net

and delayed communication but is strongly supported by scientific values and ethics. Yet, and despite its success, there are limits.

As a matter of fact open access does not solve all the problems of scientific and technical information, and it may even create others. Harnad et al. (2004) say that open repositories (the green road) may well contribute to the access/impact problem insofar as they increase the availability and potential impact (citations) of scientific output. But Harnad is rather skeptical about the "gold road", i.e. open access journals, as a sustainable solution for the affordability problem and predicts that this option rather than reduce the financial burden, shifts the problem from library budget to publishing charges. Especially as predatory publishing is a growing concern[4].

Moreover, we must be careful with generalizations of what is open and what is not. Diversity is the rule, not homogeneity. Access to scientific information is a multivariate concept with different shades of openness, ranking across a continuum from "open access" to "restricted access". A document may be open with regards to reader rights but more or less closed for reuse[5]. An institutional repository may fulfill different functions, such as long-term preservation, scientific impact or research evaluation whereas free and unrestricted access to all resources will not always be the priority. Absolute figures on repositories, journals and resources may be good indicators for the development of open access. But more insight is needed into successful models, best practices, degrees of openness, acceptance, usage and policies for a realistic understanding and evaluation of the open access movement.

Yet, this book shifts the focus to another point. Up to now, the open access movement has been most successful in the Western hemisphere. The three essential reference papers on open access, i.e. the Budapest, Berlin and Bethesda declarations were mainly prepared and supported by Western institutions, organizations and communities. Two-thirds of the repositories are hosted in Europe or North America, one third of the open access journals are published in six countries from the "global North", including the United States, Spain and the UK. As

---

4 http://www.nature.com/news/predatory-publishers-are-corrupting-open-access-1.11385

5 SPARC, PLOS, & OASPA (2012). *How Open Is It? Open Access Spectrum.* http://www.plos.org/

Jingfeng Xia (2012) from Indiana University says, open access has a "disproportionate growth" especially in developing countries, because of ICT infrastructures ("digital divide"), R&D intensity and, even more important, cultural dissimilarities, and meeting local standards appears to be a crucial condition for the development of open access.

...TO LOCAL ACTION

Knowledge production and exchange are part of the global inequalities, and many countries are virtually invisible on the map of global knowledge (Czerniewicz 2013). But what is adequate circulation of knowledge? How can technology help the spread of education and the growth of research capacities in a multipolar world? John Willinsky asserts that "innovations in open access publishing are taking place against the chilling historical backdrop of earlier efforts at instilling universal education and knowledge systems" (2006, p. 109-110).

To become sustainable, open access must adjust to local conditions and even more, be assimilated into local political and scientific culture, as a local initiative supported by local communities. In the global village, one size does not fit all. Each country, each region has its own history and tradition, with institutions, communities and economies that shape the way of future development. What works in one part of the world may fail elsewhere, especially if promoted or enforced as a new "unique model".

Open access is more than a "unique model" of how to circulate knowledge. More than a prescription of how to do things, open access is a principle, a framework for initiatives and projects aiming at fastening scientific communication and increasing online availability of research literature, freely and as reusable as possible. This is a challenge not only for technology and infrastructure, but also for politics, business and laws.

Also, even if open access to scientific information involves in the first place the academic communities, scientists, scholars, students and librarians, it is relevant to other groups, in particular those working in areas of health, welfare, education and justice, and affects other sectors, such as the publishing industry, information services, international cooperation and ICT start-ups.

The demand for open access is great in the developing world as it can contribute to solve problems of access gaps. Peter Suber, Open Access Project Director at Public Knowledge, Washington, observed that "researchers in the global south are among the most determined advocates for open access"[6]. They want it as readers, to have access to international research, but they want it as authors, too, so that their own work can be known to colleagues elsewhere. This last point is particularly important: open access is different from existing programs such as HINARI because it gives a perspective of participation and integration. Open access is not only access and consumption but also and above all, production and dissemination.

Open access is expected to facilitate the full participation of the global academic community in research and scholarship, sustained by international collaborative strategies. Thus, open access has the potential to contribute and foster local research and development. But to realize this potential and to make open access sustainable, we have to learn from each other, carefully, empathically, and focused on local needs and conditions.

Learning from emerging countries

In our multipolar world, five emerging countries, because of their large and fast-growing national economies, their demography and geographic situation, play a specific and leading role with a significant influence on regional and global affairs. These so-called BRICS[7] countries – Brazil, Russia, India, China and South Africa – represent together nearly three billion people, i.e. 40% of the world population, and 18% of the world economy.

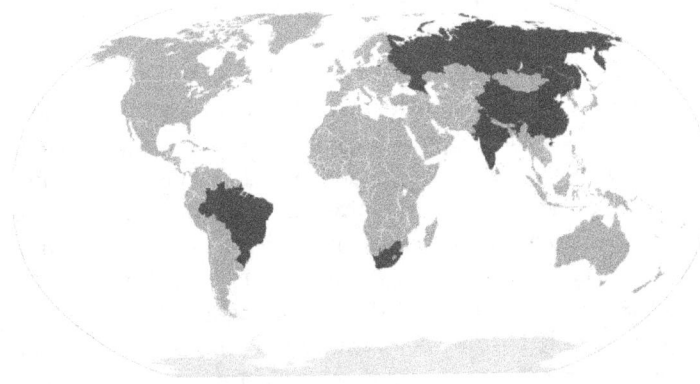

Figure 0.1: Global map of the BRICS countries (source: en.wikipedia.org)

---

6   http://poynder.blogspot.co.uk

7   The acronym BRICS was introduced by Jim O'Neill from Goldman Sachs in 2001 http://www.goldmansachs.com/our-thinking/archive/building-better.html

Their influence on global and regional affairs is commercial and financial as well as political, ecological, military and cultural, and they also stand for an increasing part of the global research and development activities. In 2013, they produced 22% of the scientific documents indexed by the international SCOPUS database, with more Chinese articles than the UK, France and Germany cumulated. Emerging today may become dominant tomorrow.

Regarding open access, they are part of the movement but their ranking is contrasted. Following the international directories for open access repositories and journals, the BRICS countries publish 17% of all open access journals (mainly Brazil and India) but host less than 10% of the open repositories. However, these figures are not exhaustive, especially for Chinese journals, and the real number of repositories and journals in the BRICS is surely higher.

At first sight, there is no specific "BRICS approach to open access". Each country developed its own policy and infrastructure of open access. Each development is very different from the others. For instance, whereas Brazil launched a central platform for open access journal publishing that gained world-wide visibility and impact, China started to transform their numerous and independent print journals into digital and freely available online products. Also, while some countries focus on regional impact, in competition with Western countries. Yet, there are examples of collaboration and partnership, especially between Brazil, India and South Africa. They work together, and they learn from each other.

The BRICS are not similar; they are far from a unique model but they offer different approaches and projects that may be models for other countries. Each local solution is a potential opportunity for tomorrow's scientific communication. Will future openness set optimal incentives for the creation of knowledge? "Many wrong paths could be picked and may result in dead-ends. It is important that stakeholders are flexible and honest enough to be able to leave dead-end streets" (Bartling & Friesike 2014, p.12). Diversity is not a problem but a chance, and it will support the sustainable development of open access. Diversity, richness of projects and mutual learning are necessary on the way to open science.

OVERVIEW

The economic situations of the emergent countries are quite different, as well as their academic system of higher education and research. Also, each country has developed different models of academic publishing for the dissemination of its research results. These models, even if partly integrated into the international market of scientific and technical information, reflect specific situations and strategies often not well known in the Western world. The value proposal of our book is to provide this information and to close a gap in scientific literature on academic publishing. The reason is twofold: not only to share with these countries a growing part of the international scientific and technical information market but also to allow them to provide interesting and alternative options for this market too. Today this market is largely dominated by American, British, Dutch and German publishers and models. Our hypothesis is that tomorrow, these models will have to share their dominant position with the emerging countries including their cultural, linguistic, scientific and economic diversity and richness. Also, these countries may be better positioned to provide sustainable models for other regions such as the Maghreb, sub-Saharan Africa or Latin America.

Our objective is to provide the reader – librarian, scientist, publisher, student or citizen interested in open science – with valuable and recent information on the open access in each of the five countries so that he/she can make up his/her mind. Therefore we asked experts, information professionals and scientists from Brazil, Russia, India, China and South Africa to describe the open access situation in their different countries for an international readership, with an empirical approach and focusing on country-specific characteristics and challenges. How are they doing, and why? Where are the bottlenecks? What can be learned? Each chapter has its particular topic and perspective:

Brazil: The first chapter presents the open access journal platform ScieELO, the most important open access server for scientific journals worldwide, with an impact well beyond Brazil.

Russia: Chapter two provides a general overview on institutional initiatives for free dissemination of public research on the Internet, especially in the field of grey literature, in a society with strong traditions of public interest prevailing on private intellectual property.

India: Along with a detailed description of the open access movement in India, the third chapter informs about awareness and acceptance of institutional repositories and open access journals among Indian scientific communities.

China: The author presents the results of a recent survey on the development of open access journals in China. This is interesting insofar as only very few titles are known and indexed outside of China.

South Africa: The last chapter shows how open access can increase its impact and also protect local content, and how it can build on African cultural traditions and values of *Ubuntu*, i.e. relatedness, sharing and generosity.

Each chapter is introduced by "Facts & Figures", a section with some basic data about each country, on its economic performance, research and development, scientific output and open access publishing. These data collected between March and September 2014, come from several sources (UNESCO Institute of Statistics, Battelle-*R&D Magazine*, ProQuest UlrichsWeb, Scopus, OpenDOAR, DOAJ, Wikipedia, Worldometers.info) and have been cross validated whenever possible. The maps have been adapted from the United Nations Office for the Coordination of Humanitarian Affairs OCHA website[8]. Moreover, this section provides a summary of the following chapter and introduces the author(s).

Each chapter tells a story, and each story is different. How can we conclude such a book? Instead of a synthesis, we asked Pierre Mounier, a historian from the School for Advanced Studies in Social Sciences in Paris, and Deputy Director of the French OpenEdition publishing house, to conduct a virtual roundtable with our authors in order to find out what is common, what is different, what can be learned and what are the threats and opportunities for the future development of open access – a real challenge but also a way to emphasize shared values and engagement in the international community of open access and open science, and to finish the book with an open debate and new perspectives.

Last but not least, we would like to thank Chérifa Boukacem-Zeghmouri (France), Ulrich Herb (Germany) and Maebena Soukouya (Togo) for helpful discussions and suggestions, Hélène Prost (France) for the preparation of the "Facts & Figures", the references and the

---

8   http://www.unocha.org

annex, Victoria Johnston (France) for English proofreading and the publisher Rory Litwin for his steady support and interest for this untypical project. A special thanks and much gratefulness for the book's authors, for their experience, knowledge, engagement and convictions. The book is dedicated to all librarians and scientists, anonymous or not, in developing and emergent countries promoting and working for open access and open science in their country and around the world.

REFERENCES

Bartling, S, & Friesike, S 2014, *Opening science,* Springer, Heidelberg.

Czerniewicz, L 2013, *Inequitable power dynamics of global knowledge production and exchange must be confronted head on,* London School of Economics. Available from: http://blogs.lse.ac.uk/impactofsocialsciences/2013/04/29/redrawing-the-map-from-access-to-participation

Harnad, S et al. 2004, 'The access/impact problem and the green and gold roads to open access', *Serials Review,* vol. 30, no. 4, pp. 310-314.

Orduña-Malea, E & Lopez-Cozar, ED 2014, 'The dark side of open access in Google and Google Scholar: the case of Latin-American repositories', Available from: http://arxiv.org/abs/1406.4331

Suber, P 2012, *Open access,* The MIT Press, Cambridge.

Willinsky, J 2005, The access principle: the case for open access to research and scholarship (digital libraries and electronic publishing), The MIT Press, Cambridge.

Xia, J 2012, 'Diffusionism and open access', *Journal of Documentation,* vol. 68, no. 1, pp. 72-99.

About the Author

Joachim Schöpfel is lecturer of Library and Information Sciences at the University of Lille 3 (France), director of the French Digitization Centre for PhD theses (ANRT) and member of the GERiiCO research laboratory. He was manager of the INIST (CNRS) scientific library from 1999 to 2008. He teaches library marketing, auditing, intellectual property and information science. His research interests are scientific information and communication, especially open access and grey literature.

Facts & Figures:
Brazil

Country and Economy

Capital	Name of Capital: Brasilía
Area	In km²: 8,514,083
Population Size	2013 Estimate: 200,361,925 Country Ranking: 5
Density	Per km²: 24
GDP (nominal)	In Billions of US$ (2014 estimate): 2,523,344 Country Ranking: 7
GDP per Capita	In US$ (2014 estimate): 12,528 Country Ranking: 69
Human Development Index	HDI (2012): 0.730 Country Ranking: 85

Research and Open Access

Scientists	Total Number (2009) (in thousand): 129.1 Per Capita: 668 per 1 million
Expenditures on Research and Development	In Billions of US$ (2011): 19.4 % of GDP: 0.9% Country Ranking: 11
Publications	Total Number (2013): 59,111 Country Ranking: 13 Number of Citable Documents: 56,017
Citations	Total Number (2013): 18,570 Country Ranking: 17 Citations per Document: 0.31 H-Index: 342
Journals	Total Number of Academic and Scholarly Journals (2014): 1,493 Journals with Impact Factor (2012): 120
Open Archives	Institutional Repositories: 66 Disciplinary Repositories: 9 Aggregating Repositories: 2 Governmental Repositories: 7
Open Access Journals	Total Number of Open Access Journals • UlrichsWeb: 1,403 • DOAJ: 936

OVERVIEW

Covering half of the surface of South America, Brazil is the largest country of Latin America, with an extraordinarily rich biodiversity. Brazil's contribution to the global movement towards open access is the SciELO (Scientific Electronic Library On-line) project. Difficult to say what exactly SciELO is: a platform for open access publishing? A digital library? An international network? It is all of this, and more than that. First started in Brazil and, shortly afterward, in Chile, SciELO has been running for more than fifteen years now. Initially launched as a server for journal publishing designed to improve the visibility of Brazilian journals on the Internet, it has become the most important and best known open access journal platform worldwide. Open access has allowed for more visibility, transparency, and credibility for the SciELO journals that now span over three continents with more than 1,000 titles from twelve countries, including Portugal, Spain and South Africa. The number of issues and articles is steadily growing, largely exceeding half a million articles in a broad range of scientific disciplines and fields.

Abel L. Packer who coordinates the SciELO program, provides a detailed insight into the history of SciELO and reveals the key factors of its success, such as international cooperation, institutional support and sponsorship, political lobbying and proactive communication, federation of stakeholders instead of isolation or competition, standardization... If today SciELO represents the most successful and impressive example of "gold" open access, that is, open access based on publishing rather than self-archiving, one reason is surely the fact that from the beginning, the project is valued and insists on high content quality and selectivity, on evaluation and scientometrics, and on indexing and metadata. Other reasons are the close partnership with research organizations together with publishers and the search for sustainability.

What can be learned is a particularly original mixture of visionary strategy towards open access and realistic, even opportunistic goal setting. But the success story does not end here, and the following chapter shows the dynamics and potential of the SciELO network and platform. More countries, like Bolivia, Paraguay and Uruguay will join the project, indexing and referencing will be improved, and the platform has started to publish books and proceedings from scientific events.

More than a simple project, SciELO is today a reference and model for other emerging and developing countries, as a specific Global South solution to open access. It is also the world's most successful alternative to commercial open access publishing with article processing charges and as such, a political message in favour of public, not-for-profit and independent academic publishing.

SciELO has entered a phase of consolidation. How will it develop the relationship with publishers? How will it work together with institutional repositories? Will the boundaries between gold and green become blurred? How will SciELO deal with mega- and overlay journals? These are open questions that will shape the future of SciELO.

About the Author

Abel L. Packer is Director of the Scientific Electronic Library Online (SciELO) Program of the São Paulo Research Foundation (FAPESP) and Advisor on Information and Communication on Science at the Foundation of the Federal University of São Paulo (UNIFESP), Brazil, since June 2010. Previously he was Director of the Latin American and Caribbean Center on Health Sciences (BIREME) of the Pan American Health Organization/World Health Organization for 11 years. He participated pro-actively in the conception, management, operation and dissemination of major Latin American and Caribbean multilingual scientific information networks, such as the Latin American Population Documentation System (DOCPAL), the Virtual Health Library (VHL) and the Scientific Electronic Library Online. Mr. Packer holds a bachelor degree in Sciences and a Master Degree in Library Sciences.

The SciELO Program and Gold Road Open Access

Abel L. Packer

Introduction

Latin America and the Caribbean is the region of the world which, proportionally speaking, publishes more of its scientific research in open access (OA). For 2013, the Web of Science Core Collection (WoS) showed that some 11% of the 1.6 million articles indexed in this database were published in OA. USA contributes with some 9% of its articles and Western Europe with 11% whereas Latin America boasts an impressive 27%, with Brazil leading the region with approximately one third of its articles available in OA. In July 2014, Brazil was out on its own in first place in the Directory of Open Access Journals as far as the number of OA articles was concerned.

The performance of Brazil and the other countries of Latin America and the Caribbean can be mainly attributed to both nationally and regionally published journals, the majority of which are published in OA. For example, in 2013, of the total number of articles published in journals from Brazil indexed in WoS, 73% were in OA. This predominance of OA journals can be observed in the catalog of the 20,875 active journals indexed in Scopus in June 2014. 12% of these journals are published in OA, a figure which rises to 65% for the Latin American and Caribbean region, 70% for Brazil and 80% for Chile.

In true pioneering spirit, OA was adopted by the Scientific Electronic Library Online Program (SciELO) in 1998 under the leadership of Brazil and Chile, with the objective of promoting the visibility and online availability of full text, as well as the use and impact of research communicated by means of quality nationally published journals (Packer 2009). This adoption of OA in 1998 took place 4 years before the OA movement was formalized by the Budapest Declaration. The predominance of OA in Latin America and the Caribbean in association with the SciELO Program is recognized in the international scientific and technical literature (Miguel et al. 2011)[1].

First and foremost, this chapter describes the background history which contributed to the rise of SciELO, the pioneering adoption of OA and its consolidation as the "modus operandi" for the publication of the network of SciELO journal collections published in Latin America and the Caribbean, Spain, Portugal and South Africa; secondly, it will provide an outline of the development of the SciELO model which comprises the integration of the functions of indexing, publication and interoperability of journals and the articles they contain; thirdly, it will analyze critical aspects in journal evolution within the context of SciELO and the strengths, barriers and major challenges that must be faced to improve quality and keep abreast of the state of the art in scholarly communication; and fourthly, it will list the major lines of action which will guide the future development of SciELO and its journals.

The chapter will conclude by stressing that OA will continue to predominate as far as the future publication of SciELO journals is concerned, but that its development and qualification will depend, in part, on the success achieved by the refinements which are being promoted by the SciELO Program and the capacity for renewal on the part of publishers and journal editors. This success will, however, be decisively influenced by the capacity of national research evaluation systems to place an appropriate value on the vital role which is typically carried out by the majority of nationally published journals[2].

---

1   See also Science Matrix. Proportion of open access peer-reviewed papers at the European and World levels–2004-2011 http://www.science-metrix.com/pdf/SM_EC_OA_Availability_2004-2011.pdf.

2   A more complete overview of SciELO is presented in the book *SciELO – 15 Years of Open Access* co-published by UNESCO and SciELO (Packer et al. 2014).

THE ORIGINS AND CONSOLIDATION OF GOLD ROAD OA IN THE LATIN AMERICAN AND CARIBBEAN REGION

The conditions which brought about the large-scale adoption of OA by quality journals published in Latin America and the Caribbean are the products of two convergent movements. First and foremost, a coming together of international and regional policies and programs supporting the development of the management of information and scholarly communication which took place over the last forty years. Secondly, these efforts were carried out within the context of or in convergence or in partnership with national policies and programs for fostering research, scholarly communication and the translation of scientific knowledge in support of teaching, professional practice and informing public policies. Within these programs, the support of nationally published journals based on the evaluation of their performance played a key role.

International cooperation

Specialized bodies of the United Nations, in particular the following, have all established very effective and innovative programs of technical cooperation among the national institutions which support research and scholarly communication in the countries of the Latin American and Caribbean region:

- The Economic Commission for Latin America and the Caribbean (ECLAC) through its Latin American Centre for Economic and Social Documentation (CLADES) that led to the development of the ECLAC Bibliographic Format and the Latin American and Caribbean Demographic Center (CELADE) through its Population Documentation System (DOCPAL);

- UNESCO through its Information for All Program (IFAP) and the actions of its regional offices in the Latin American and Caribbean region;

- the Food and Agricultural Organization through its International System for Agricultural Science and Technology office (AGRIS);

- the Inter-American Institute for Cooperation on Agriculture (IICA) / Tropical Agriculture Research and Education Center

(CATIE) through the Alliance of Agricultural Information and Documentation Services of the Americas (SIDALC);

- the International Atomic Energy Agency (IAEA) through its International Nuclear Information System (INIS);
- the World Health Organization (WHO) through its regional office for the Americas, the Pan-American Health Organization (PAHO), and its Latin American and Caribbean Centre on Health Sciences Information, more commonly known as BIREME which is derived from its Spanish and Portuguese original name –the Biblioteca Regional de Medicina.

The technical cooperation programs were oriented towards the development of national competencies and infrastructures on information and scholarly communication. These programs contributed to meeting the growing demand for scientific information from teaching and research communities which were not fully served by the collections of libraries located in institutions of teaching and research in their countries, and these programs contributed to the establishment of bibliographic control of scientific, technical and governmental output in countries within the region, by means of indexing systems based on subject disciplines aligned with the major international subject indexes listed above.

In this process, technical cooperation programs addressed the critical question of contextualizing the international evolution of information systems, products and services to national and regional conditions and requirements. At the same time, these programs helped to fine-tune and bring about innovations in methodologies and technologies for the management and operation of information sources and processes with the progressive use of information and communication technologies. This happened first of all at the end of the 1960s and the start of the 1970s with the reduced use of mainframes and minicomputers, followed by the use of desktop computers in standalone mode or working within local networks, and from the 1990s with the progressive adoption of the Internet.

Cost-free availability, along with a comprehensive training and technical support program at both the national and regional level for the desktop computer software package CDS/ISIS from UNESCO, designed for the storage and retrieval of structured text, and especially bibliographic records, was instrumental in educating thousands of librarians and information professionals in the management and automated operation of catalogs and making the automation of libraries and scientific information centers and services more viable. International databases also began to be operated on a national basis by means of the CDS/ISIS software.

In addition, in collaboration with programs of cooperation in scientific information from the United Nations, many information-related institutions as well as agencies and foundations from the developed world that supported development made a decisive contribution to the advancement of the management and operation of scientific information sources in the Latin American and Caribbean region. Among these, it is important to highlight the significant contributions made by the United States National Library of Medicine (NLM), the Kellogg Foundation and the Canadian International Development Research Centre (IDRC).

These policies and regional programs made progress by providing answers to problems, demands and the common expectations held by the countries of the region towards the development of national capabilities and infrastructures in line with the state of the art internationally speaking in this regard, and were favored by the coming together of political, social, economic and cultural factors, including the predominant position of the Spanish and Portuguese languages, which, on many occasions, presented serious barriers to accessing information and keeping up with the international state of the art in the management of information and scholarly communication.

Networking

A determining characteristic of these policies, programs and projects was the central position played by national and regional networks of institutions with libraries, information centers and services, and scholarly communication. The networks were progressively constructed using common practices, and asserted themselves as the "modus operandi" of cooperation, division of labor, and construction of a critical mass of accessible collections of content and user communities, professionals and institutions linked with the production and intermediation of scientific information and contributed towards the adoption of standards and common or compatible operating platforms.

Working in a network brings with it well known advantages such as accelerated advancement promoted by mutual exchange, sharing of information, knowledge, resources and content. At the same time however, this way of working faces challenges which derive mainly from the complexity of the management of different asymmetries and priorities in an undertaking of shared objectives which presupposes a minimal level of equity in participation. In this way neutrality, in the face of national conditions and circumstances, favored the action of international organizations as well as developed countries' agencies in overcoming many of the complexities involved in the introduction of innovations, and played a decisive role in the development of information and communication networks in Latin America and the Caribbean region. However, it is also certain that inconsistencies in international and country agencies' policies for technical cooperation, produced as a consequence of the growing constraint on resources, the inability to innovate, changes in priorities with regard to the support of development, and absence of or change in leadership at the highest levels of research and scientific information had put the brake on or interrupted the rhythm of development in networks in the Latin American and Caribbean region, in many cases before their operation could be consolidated and adopted by the countries themselves. In many cases, the increasing availability and interoperability of information sources on the Web contributed to and/or overcame the weakening of the traditional institutional-based networks.

The Virtual Health Library (VHL) network which was made up of hundreds of libraries and scientific information centers in the health field, covering practically all the institutes of research, education and health care situated in Latin America and the Caribbean with close relationships to the major scientific information systems worldwide, and with particular emphasis on those which are coordinated by the NLM, WHO and the UNESCO, is an example of the evolution of cooperative networks and of its positive legacy for institutions and national systems of scientific information.

The setting up and development of the VHL at the end of the 1990s was a synthesis of the advances made in policy, methodology and technology contributed by the different networks and international programs of cooperation, and forms an integral part of the history of the evolution of more than 40 years of technical cooperation of BIREME both within the Latin American and Caribbean region and with other developing regions of the world, especially in Africa.

The role of BIREME

The activity of BIREME was always carried out through network mechanisms and the adoption, adaptation and development of successive waves of methodologies and technical developments in information technologies in order to respond to the conditions and demands of countries from Latin America and the Caribbean. BIREME moved forward, supported by the close partnership of PAHO/WHO with the government of Brazil, through the Ministries of Education and Health, the Government of the State of São Paulo and the Federal University of São Paulo (UNIFESP) that host BIREME's headquarters. It began its operation in 1967 with the establishment of a document delivery service which offered access to photocopies of articles published in scientific journals taken from paper-based journal collections shared by an extensive national and international network involving hundreds of libraries.

Since the end of the 1960s, BIREME operated the MEDLINE database, first from the facilities of the Institute of Energy and Nuclear Research (IPEN), affiliated with the University of São Paulo, and subsequently from its own computer facilities and acting as one of the MEDLARS Centers established worldwide by the NLM. Within a few years, it supplemented the availability of access to MEDLINE for the countries in Latin America and the Caribbean with the creation of a regional bibliographic index with the objective of establishing a comprehensive bibliographic control and dissemination of the health related scientific and technical literature from Latin America and the Caribbean. Initially, this bibliographic index published on paper and entitled the Index Medicus Latino-Americano (IMLA) only covered scientific journals. Subsequently, as part of a third phase in the operation of the cooperative network, the indexing process was expanded to include all document types under the name of the Latin American and Caribbean Health Sciences Literature database (LILACS). It became operational in a decentralized manner with each individual country assuming responsibility for recording its own scientific literature, initially in paper form, for input into LILACS type databases operated on microcomputers, and subsequently in an automated fashion with the use of desktop computers. During this phase, BIREME created the Latin American and Caribbean System for Information on Health Sciences as the management and operation framework of its network of libraries and centers of scientific and technical information. It was also during this phase that BIREME pioneered the use of CD-ROM technology in the developing world with the launching in 1987 of the LILACS/CD-ROM to distribute the LILACS database and later the MEDLINE to its network.

Online development

With the emergence of the Internet and the progressive consolidation of the Web as the new media of scholarly communication, the network national leaderships under the coordination of BIREME, moved the cooperation modus operandi forward to a fourth phase which focused on operating online using the Web with the creation of the VHL in 1998 after the Declaration of San José Towards the Virtual Health Library. This online library network was set up as a comprehensive and innovative program of technical cooperation designed according to three major dimensions (Packer & Castro 1998)[3].

The first dimension has a political character and encompasses a strategy for the democratization of access and publication of scientific information as a central condition and social determinant of health. The organization and publication of research outputs of the countries of the region and their inclusion in the international flow of scholarly information is prioritized alongside the access to international research output. It is in this political dimension that the origins of OA in the region were shaped.

The second dimension, which deals with issues of methodology and standardization, is the network approach to managing scientific and technical information and knowledge based on multidisciplinary and multilingual commons involving librarianship, information science and IT, and management disciplines.

The third dimension, which has an operational character, consists of the practical implementation of the VHL by means of three types of converging networks: firstly, social networks consisting of producers, intermediaries and users of scientific information (note that the concept of social network was originally defined and restricted to institutional and personal relationships within the scope of the VHL and before it acquired the broad nature on the Web around centralized universal systems of interaction among users); secondly, networks of content (or information sources) operated online on the Web; and

---

[3] See also VHL Guide. São Paulo: BIREME/PAHO/WHO, March 2011. 45p.

thirdly, networks of learning and informed environments centered on the management of local information flows based on the exchange of information and experiences between local players interacting with the VHL space.

The online library, in the face of a variety of products, services and collections of scientific and technical documents made viable by the Web, in addition to the traditional types of paper-based documents, was functionally structured in accordance with six different types of information sources:

- Primary sources, which mainly consist of collections of online full text documents.

- Secondary sources, which are composed of metadata indexes with online access to full text or to photocopying services wherever possible.

- The third type of information sources are aimed at education and decision making with an emphasis on systematic reviews such as the Cochrane Library.

- The fourth type comprised the selective dissemination of information.

- The fifth, the communication systems and online spaces of cooperation.

- And, lastly, the methodologies and technologies which support the operation of the library.

For each type of information source, the VHL considers the development of a methodological framework and one or more operational networks (involving network of producers, intermediaries and users, a network of contents, and networks of informed learning environments), which became known as associate networks of the VHL.

Among these associated networks, the following instances were directly related to the advancement of research and were developed by means of projects and specific alliances and partnerships with national research agencies: the Scientific Electronic Library Online (SciELO) which was developed as primary information source encompassing online full text digital versions of scientific journals, and the International Network for the Management of Sources of Information and Knowledge in Support of the Management of Science, Technology and Innovation (ScienTI) as a primary source of researchers' CVs and of research groups, based on the Lattes Platform of CVs of Brazilian affiliated researchers led by the National Council for Scientific and Technological Development (CNPq) of Brazil. These networks were characterized thematically, politically and administratively by reaching out beyond the health field, which is the focus of the VHL, and no longer represented by ministries of health and education but rather by national science, technology and innovation-related agencies and councils.

Launching SciELO to improve journal visibility

As mentioned above, the major challenge of ensuring the political, financial, managerial and operational sustainability of the cooperative networks and of the continuity of their methods, products and services was always found to be making viable the transition of the coordination and management by international bodies to the responsibility of the countries. In the case of ScienTI and SciELO VHL associate networks, this transition started in 2008 with the transference of the network political and operational leadership to Colombia and Brazil research agencies, respectively. ScienTI network did not succeed to survive but nevertheless its legacy remained in terms of capabilities and national infrastructures. However, the SciELO network was very successful in this transition due to the competence and leadership on scholarly communication of the Foundations and Councils of Science and Technology in the countries concerned.

The SciELO Program had its beginnings in 1997 and developed as a result of the partnership between BIREME and the São Paulo Research Foundation (FAPESP), an agency which celebrated its fiftieth anniversary in 2012. Annually, this organization disburses some US 500 million dollars to the advancement of research in the state of São Paulo, which produces half of the science output of Brazil as measured by the number of articles indexed internationally.

At the time when SciELO was created, FAPESP had been maintaining a regular program of financial support of selected scientific journals published in the State of São Paulo for more than a decade. This complemented the federal programs headed up by CNPq and the Brazilian Innovation Agency (FINEP). The FAPESP and the federal programs evolved on the basis of the results obtained from evaluation studies of journals from Brazil, which were carried out for guiding financial support and as academic research (Krzyzanowski & Ferreira 1998; Ribeiro et al. 2007).

The methodologies which underpinned the evaluation of research journals in Brazil were adopted and perfected from experiences in Latin America which went back to 1962 with the drafting of the Latin American Guide to Scientific and Technical Journal Publications (Guía de Publicaciones Periódicas Científicas y Técnicas de América Latina) by the Panamerican Union–Centre of Scientific and Technical Documentation (Centro de Documentación Científica y Técnica de México). In 1964, the Working Group for the Selection of Latin-American Scientific Journals met in Puerto Rico under the coordination of UNESCO. The evolution of the recommendations of this Working Group contributed to the continued progress of the bibliographic control of journals published in Latin America and the Caribbean and culminated in the establishment in 1997 of the Latindex control and registration system for periodicals published in the Ibero-American countries (Cetto& Alonso-Gamboa 1998).

In 1985, FAPESP set up a coordinating unit for publications which developed a ranking system for peer reviewed journals published in Brazil with the aim of defining a core collection for which support could be granted in the face of the growing number of requests for funding that FAPESP was receiving. This assessment was updated in 1990 with the analysis and ranking of 2,215 journals in all subject disciplines. Of these, 372 (17%) were considered to be relevant to the core collection (Krzyzanowski et al. 1991). A similar ranking system was developed at the federal level by CNPq.

These evaluations acted as a benchmark for SciELO when it began to define its initial core collection. The models, criteria and indicators used in these evaluations measured journals' performance with respect to the openness and representative nature of their editorial bodies related to their disciplines and research communities, their ability to publish in terms of quantity, timeliness of publication, and quality of the articles on the basis of the evaluation of researchers who were representative of the subject areas covered by each particular journal.

The evaluations and their respective rankings fostered a growing necessity for editorial improvement and self-evaluation by publishing institutions and journal editors alike. In connection with this, the Brazilian Association of Scientific Editors (ABEC) was set up in 1985 and has been steadily working since that date with the objective of making a contribution to scholarly communication in Brazil and to the training and updating of journal editors in all disciplines. No other country in the Latin American and Caribbean region can count on such a forum of journal editors where the different questions which have an impact on editorial policy and scholarly communication can be discussed.

Nevertheless, except for the small number of 17 Brazilian journals included up until 1998 in the citation indexes of the then Institute of Scientific Information (ISI), these evaluations were not taking into account the performance of the journals and of their articles by the number of citations they were receiving (Meneghini 1998).

THE DEVELOPMENT OF THE SciELO MODEL

The partnership between FAPESP and BIREME which gave rise to the SciELO Program owed its origin to the convergence of their respective priority action lines for the development of scientific journals.

On BIREME's side, the VHL foresaw the development of a primary information source of full texts with a particular emphasis on journal content. On FAPESP's side, the policy of journal support required improvement in the evaluation of journals with an interest in establishing an index of citations of journals from Brazil which would complement the ISI indexes and, in particular, the bibliometric indicators found in the Journal Citation Reports (JCR) (Packer et al. 2014).

Financial and administrative management

FAPESP financed a pilot research project which was drawn up in conjunction with BIREME to develop methodologies and technologies for the online indexing and publication of full text journals. This pilot project took place between February 1997 and March 1998 with 10 journals covering various subjects and disciplines, and whose editors-in-chief acted as the advisory group for the pilot project, holding regular meetings with the project technical team.

After the success of this pilot project, FAPESP directed its political and financial support to the development and operation of the SciELO Program as a Special Research Program with grants which would be renewed every 2 or 3 years under the scientific coordination of a principal researcher and a dedicated team. The operation counted upon the leadership and active participation of BIREME which, as mentioned before, promoted the development of the SciELO journal collections as an associate network of the VHL, notwithstanding the fact that the SciELO collection would encompass different areas of scientific knowledge with around one third of the journals in the health sciences field.

With the launching of the regular operation of SciELO as of March 1998, the SciELO model was adopted in that same year by the National Commission for Scientific and Technical Research (CONICYT) in Chile, thereby giving rise to the SciELO Network (Prat, 2000; Packer et al. 2014). From 2002, CNPq also began its cooperation with SciELO by providing research funding on an annual basis. In that same year, a partnership between BIREME and CNPq was also set up for the development of the ScienTI network, under the regional leadership of the Unit for the Promotion and Development of Research of PAHO.

The transition of the responsibility of the coordination and operation of the SciELO Program to Brazil under the leadership of FAPESP was carried out with the coming together of institutional infrastructure, human resources, and a physical and connectivity infrastructure provided by different entities affiliated to UNIFESP. As of 2008, the execution of research funding provided by CNPq and the FAPESP SciELO Program was gradually carried out by the UNIFESP Foundation (FapUNIFESP), and this became firmly established as of 2010. The transition of the management of the ScienTI network had already been finalized in 2009 with the transfer of its management to the Administrative Department for Science, Technology and Innovation of Colombia (COLCIENCIAS).

The establishment of the SciELO Program for the development of quality journals edited and published by national institutions dovetailed with an action line which, as described for Brazil above, was common to practically all national research councils in the countries of Latin America. Nevertheless, the comprehensive nature and level of funding of these action lines varied from country to country and without the characteristics of public policies per se with goals and budgets established by national research plans. In the majority of cases, the action lines combined the evaluation of the past performance of journals with the provision of financial assistance which was limited to maintaining the continuity of the publication of the most distinguished journals in a particular country. These action lines were characterized by the reaction to the demands and pressures of the entities responsible for the journals and their editors, and rarely aimed at the improvement of the journals themselves. The SciELO Program was an innovation in this regard and brought to the table a coherent and forward-looking set of objectives, methodologies and technologies which demonstrated a noteworthy contribution to the renewal of national journal support programs.

Improving visibility

The major objective behind the establishment of the SciELO Program remains unchanged: making a key contribution to maximizing national and international visibility, use and impact of journals published by national institutions by means of their indexing, publication and online interoperability on the Web, organized in national collections published in gold road OA without embargo.

In 1997, the adoption of online publication and OA went forward with a high degree of pioneering spirit. The Program developed the SciELO Model, made up of three important and dynamic components:

- first and foremost, a methodological and technical platform for the indexing, publication and online interoperability of journals;

- secondly, a governance and management guide for the establishment, operation and evaluation of national and thematic journal collections whose management, financing and operation are the responsibility of each country;

- and, thirdly, the shaping of the SciELO Network of national and thematic collections following a common methodological and technical platform.

The Network is represented in and is accessible via the SciELO global portal[4]. The network has evolved with each nationally managed and financed collection, and with all collections following the same principles and methodological and technical platform.

The SciELO proposal tackled head on the recurring problem of lack of visibility, and often before a good part of the journals published in the Latin American and Caribbean countries became aware of it. This lack of visibility was perceived and determined, on the one hand, by

---

4   http://www.scielo.org

the limited presence of the journals in the international bibliographic indexes, and on the other hand, by the limited number of editions, a low number of subscribers and high distribution costs by mail. In the particular case of Brazil, when SciELO was created, as we have seen above, less than 20 journals had bibliometric indicators in JCR, that is, 5% of Brazilian journals were considered to be relevant according to the FAPESP evaluation criteria. This low coverage in the international indexes represented a barrier to the progress of the journals as vehicles for the publication of advanced research. Proposals and perspectives in favor of the better indexing of journals were not moving forward since they were bogged down by the well-known vicious circle or Catch 22 problem: since the journals had not been indexed, they were not receiving quality article submissions and were therefore not meeting the criteria required for indexing. Another critical limitation was found in the fact that the majority of journals published in Latin America and the Caribbean published research outputs in Spanish and Portuguese which offered little scope for international exposure. A good proportion of the journals were also slow to publish.

Bibliographic control and bibliometrics

These problems were largely solved by SciELO when it set itself up as a selective bibliographic index for quality journals in all subject disciplines, operating through national indexing centers knowledgeable of the characteristics of these disciplines, academic societies, the capabilities of research groups and of the serious nature of the management of journals.

As an index of bibliographical control, SciELO's proposition could be considered as an extension of the existing subject indexes of journals in the region, highlighting such examples as the CLASE (Latin American Citations in the Social Sciences and Humanities) and PERIODICA (Index of Latin American Journals in the Sciences) indexes produced by the General Directorate of Libraries at Universidad Autonoma de México (UNAM), DOCPAL (Latin American Population Documentation System) which is produced by the United Nations Latin American Centre for Demographics of the Economic Commission for Latin America and the Caribbean (ECLAC), and LILACS (Latin American and Caribbean Literature in the Health Sciences) which is produced by BIREME. But SciELO came into existence with a proposition that, politically and operationally speaking, was far more comprehensive, innovative and qualified than the indexes mentioned earlier.

SciELO consists of three dimensions which comprehensively enrich the mechanisms of bibliographic control, promote the visibility of both articles and journals, and enable the evaluation of their usage as measured by the number of downloads, and of their impact as measured by the number of citations received.

The first dimension is that of indexing which consists of the generation of the metadata records for the journal articles. This also includes a record for each one of the bibliographic references of the citations made in the articles following the model of the ISI citation indexes; the second dimension is the publication of the full-text which consists of the structuring and storage of its elements in databases for availability online, with the management and counting of citations to and from articles, as well as the number of accesses to and downloads of the articles themselves; and, the third dimension is interoperability which consists of links and the interchange of the metadata of the journals and the articles with systems, indexers and Web browsers.

This integrated, pioneering approach, which is peculiar to SciELO, simultaneously involving as it does, the functions of indexing, publication and interoperability, was the decisive factor in its success, along with the agencies and foundations of research support, publishers and editors, researchers, professors, students and the public in general.

SciELO produces bibliometric indicators from the records of the bibliographic references cited by the articles which, despite being restricted to the universe of journals in the SciELO collections, nevertheless allow for the monitoring of the performance of the journals through citations from national journals, and progressively by way of citations from SciELO journals of other countries. In this way, SciELO positioned itself as an index with a broad coverage of journals from Latin America and the Caribbean, and complementary to the JCR index and SCOPUS.

In providing the journals with a common up-to-date solution, and at no cost, SciELO made the wide adoption of online publishing viable at a time when there was a lot of resistance to the adoption of digital publishing and the Web as a medium for scholarly communication, when there were few and limited technical solutions, and financial constraints for the development of in-house solutions. In providing content interoperability on the Web, SciELO broadened and bolstered the inclusion of its journals in the international flows of scholarly communication. For example, working with MEDLINE in the online delivery of metadata reduced the time between the publication of new issues and their indexing by several months. Exposing the metadata to harvesters with the backlinks to the article full text, and exporting it to various Web indexes provided a mechanism that solved once and for all the classic problem of access to the full text of the region's journals indexed in the international indexes. It was in this new context that the indexing of the SciELO full texts by Google Scholar generated a sudden, radical and growing increase in the number of accesses to the full text of the articles, a phenomenon that overcame the difficulties in the distribution of the texts in print form, and opened up a huge market of readers. The performance of the journals by number of accesses and downloads of their full text proved how right it was to publish in OA.

Benchmark index

Another decisive factor in the consolidation of the role of SciELO in the flows of scholarly communication was its progressive inclusion, along with WoS and PubMed, as a benchmark index for the qualification of journals in the national systems for the evaluation of research programs, groups of researchers, and research institutions. This inclusion of SciELO was first carried out in Brazil by the Qualis system of the Coordination for the Improvement of Higher Education Personnel (CAPES) of the Ministry of Education. Qualis evaluates and ranks the intellectual production of graduate programs (Souza & Paula 2002). Later, Chile included SciELO in the evaluation of the academic production of its universities which is an indicator for financing.

Even though being indexed in SciELO has a lower ranking than in WoS, SciELO's position as a benchmark index in research evaluation systems broadened and strengthened the visibility of SciELO among researchers as an alternative to WoS. For those journals that were already indexed internationally, SciELO represented an important contribution to the online availability of journals' full texts. The consequence of SciELO being recognized as a benchmark index began to be reflected by an increase in the number of article submissions to the journals indexed in SciELO, such that indexing became a critical issue for the future advancement of journals from Brazil and progressively of the other countries in the SciELO Network.

In January 2014 the SciELO Program concluded an agreement with Thomson Reuters for the inclusion of the SciELO Citation Index (SciELO CI) in the Web of Science platform. In addition to the visibility that the Web of Science brings, SciELO CI will include the counts of citations received by SciELO articles from the universe of journals in the Web of Science, thus overcoming the prior limitation of counting citations restricted to the universe of journals indexed in SciELO. In other words, SciELO journals not indexed in WoS will have citations counted that come from journals in the universe of journals indexed in the WoS, and the journals indexed in WoS will have citations counted that they receive from SciELO journals not indexed in WoS. With this new combined universe of citations, the SciELO Program will be able to work with indicators that are more representative of both the journals with a national focus and those with an international one.

In summary, the origin and consolidation of gold road OA as the principal publication model for journals from Latin America came about as a result of:

the policies and programs of technical cooperation in scholarly information via cooperative networks of national institutions promoted by UN agencies, and by agencies and foundations from developed countries in convergence or alliance;

the SciELO Program and its comprehensive model for indexing, online publishing and interoperability of journals through the national journal collections developed according to quality criteria.

Decisive role of Brazil

Most countries took active part in this movement, in one way or another, through their councils and foundations that support research and, in particular, through their national networks of academic libraries and information centers. However, it is important to note the decisive role of Brazil in favor of OA in the development of networks of scholarly information and, in particular, the SciELO Network.

First and foremost, Brazil led the way through its Ministries of Health, Department of Health of the State of São Paulo and UNIFESP, and financed, jointly with PAHO/ WHO, the operation of BIREME and the development of the VHL (Virtual Health Library) favoring the democratization of access to scholarly information and knowledge through advanced methodologies and technologies tailored to country conditions. Secondly, it led the way through São Paulo Research Foundation (FAPESP) for the most part, but also with the support of CNPq in promoting, leading and financing the development of the SciELO Program through the SciELO Brazil Collection since 1997. SciELO Brazil serves as the Technical Secretariat of the SciELO Network, and is responsible for the maintenance and development of the SciELO methodological and technical platform for the network. Besides its political position within the network, its financing and international cooperation, Brazil makes a decisive contribution with more than 50% of the research output communicated by the journals of the SciELO Network.

The principles that guided the adoption and development of OA in Latin America and the Caribbean, and in particular in the carrying out of the SciELO Program, were explicitly stated in the Salvador Declaration on Open Access: The Developing World Perspective. This declaration was drafted as a recommendation of the International Seminar: Open Access for Developing Countries, organized by BIREME and held in Salvador, Brazil on September 21-22, 2005 (Salvador Declaration, 2005), as part of a set of remarkable events which testified to the strength of the cooperative networks in scholarly information in Latin America and the Caribbean, especially in the Health Sciences: the 9th World Congress on Health Information and Libraries (ICML9)[5], the 7th Regional Congress on Information in Health Sciences (CRICS7), the 4th Regional Coordination Meeting of the Virtual Health Library, and the 2nd World Congress of CDS/ISIS users.

The Salvador Declaration reaffirms the significance and importance of OA for the advancement of research and education, and for cultural and economic development, particularly for developing countries and for their active participation in the global flows of scholarly information[6]. The declaration highlights the contributions made by OA to the principle of equality. Without specifically naming SciELO,

---

5   See ICML9(2005) Commitment to Equity http://www.icml.org/?lang=en

6   Salvador Declaration on Open Access: the developing world perspective (2005) http://www.icml9.org/public/documents/pdf/en/Dcl-Salvador-OpenAccess-en.pdf

the declaration recalls pioneering OA initiatives in developing countries and states that these countries should actively participate in the global movement.

From 2001, the SciELO Network expanded beyond Latin America with the entry of Spain whose collection covers journals in the health sciences. Subsequently, in 2004, Portugal adopted the SciELO model, and South Africa in 2009. The thematic collection SciELO Public Health includes two journals published by the WHO, one from the USA and another from Italy. Table 1 summarizes the make-up of the SciELO Network in 2014, indicating the date each collection began operating, the current number of journals, the number of articles and other types of documents published in 2013, and the cumulative number of articles. The SciELO Social Sciences collection, which envisaged special editions of English translations of selected articles from SciELO journals in the Social Sciences with the objective of increasing their visibility, was suspended in 2010 for lack of financing.

The journals in the SciELO Network–the case of Brazil

The journals have a framework in the SciELO Program that makes possible, and then broadens out, their inclusion in the national and global flows of scholarly information. SciELO represents a guarantee of quality for the journals it indexes. This guarantee differentiates them from other journals in the universe of journals of the countries that participate in the network, and is supported by a multi-faceted performance monitoring system and a policy of adoption of innovations in scholarly communication.

The Latindex reference source gives an idea of the universe of journals of the countries in the SciELO Network, and the proportion indexed by SciELO. Latindex establishes bibliographic control of Ibero-American journals according to qualification criteria. In July 2014, it registered a total of 5,512 journals published in Latin America and the Caribbean. Of this universe of journals, the SciELO Network indexed 868 journals in July 2014, in other words, less than 20% of the total number of journals registered in Latindex. A similar proportion occurs in the case of Brazil whose collection, along with Chile's, is the most developed in the network.

The Qualis system of the Ministry of Education of Brazil, another reference source, classifies journals into 8 relevancy groups with a total of more than 1,200 journals in the first four groups, of which SciELO Brazil indexes 279 (22%).

Journal publishers have complete autonomy in their editorial policies and management once these are qualified and bolstered by being indexed by SciELO. This condition of the SciELO Program, whose operation is extended out by way of the national journal collections, places it as an international public good supported by the infrastructures of scientific research of the countries participating in the network. It is a public good in the sense that it provides a common platform of services for indexing, publishing and the interoperability of journals, placed at the service of the institutions responsible for their publication, and their corresponding editors, authors and, above all, their readers.

The expectations of the SciELO Program are for the improvement of the performance of the journals in two aspects. The first is to fulfill the indexing criteria to remain in the collection which includes, among other criteria, transparency in editorial management and timely publication of the full texts in OA. The second is to increase the visibility, influence and impact of the research the journals publish.

The development of the major part of the SciELO journals, however, is historically influenced by two principal factors. The first is the lack of professionalism which prevails in editorial management, in the production of the journals and in their business models. The second is the low international impact as measured by citations received in WoS and Scopus which are used as benchmarks by research agencies to rank the performance of the journals and of the research they publish. These factors, well known by systems of national research and scholarly communication, are discussed briefly below based on the journals from Brazil and are compared with journals from the BRICS countries using data from previous studies (Packer 2014).

The Brazil Collection

The SciELO Brazil Collection is the oldest collection of the SciELO Network and has the broadest coverage with close to 30% of the total of journals in all collections and more than 40% of journals published annually. The inclusion and retention of journals in a collection are governed by policies, procedures and evaluation criteria which are applied to the journals by a scientific committee and regularly updated to reflect the progress and priorities of the SciELO Program.

The coverage of the SciELO collection differs significantly from those of WoS and Scopus. In early 2014 these three indexes covered 400 journals, of which only 25% were present in all three indexes. In 2013, out of the total of 141 journals from Brazil indexed in WoS, 101 (72%) were indexed simultaneously in WoS and in the SciELO Brazil collection of 278 journals. In the case of Scopus, out of the total of 313 journals from Brazil indexed, 197 journals (62%) were indexed simultaneously in SciELO Brazil and in Scopus.

Looking in the other direction, 36% of the journals in the SciELO Brazil collection were also indexed in WoS, and 71% also in Scopus. Journals from Brazil indexed in either WoS or Scopus but not in SciELO either do not meet the SciELO criteria or do not publish in OA.

SciELO journals are not-for-profit and are published independently by national institutions that form part of national education and research systems. In the case of Brazil, universities and their departments of research and education publish 51% of the journals indexed in SciELO Brazil. Scholarly societies and professional associations account for 33% and public institutions that are not universities yet related to research and development account for 14%. A very small number of journals are published or co-published by large international publishers. This has been increasing in the last few years with the more active presence of large commercial publishers in the Latin American market.

Editorial policies and management are, in general, conducted by each journal publisher within its own context under the leadership of researchers that dedicate a limited portion of their time to the function of editor, and rely upon the support of the teams and infrastructures provided by the responsible institutions. There are exceptionally few universities, scholarly societies or publishing institutions that have well defined editorial policies and editorial teams dedicated to the management of a range of journals. The management of the 278 journals indexed in SciELO Brazil as of the end of 2013 is distributed across 176 different institutions, in other words, an average of 1.5 journals per institution. This spread of management makes the creation of economies of scale difficult and this seriously limits the rationalization of resources and innovations.

Journal production costs are, in general, covered by a combination of sources that are principally comprised of contributions from the institutions responsible for the journals and research agencies. The levying of article processing charges is growing, above all in Brazil. However, except in a few cases, journals do not have stable financial models and need to draw up their budgets every year.

Within this operational framework, the SciELO journals perform an important function in the national systems of research and education, mainly over the last two decades. These journals complement the journals of international standing from the developed countries in communicating a significant proportion of the research in their subject disciplines and academic and institutional contexts.

International impact

The case of Brazil shows the importance of nationally published journals in the communication of national research indexed internationally. In fact, 83% of the articles published by journals from Brazil indexed in WoS in 2012 are from authors with a Brazilian affiliation. This is the highest percentage of articles from national authors in the journals of the BRICS countries indexed in WoS in 2012. This is followed by a national authorship of 81% in journals from China, 79% from Russia, 66% from South Africa and 59 % from India.

The SciELO journals, especially those from Brazil, represent a significant proportion of the articles indexed in WoS, Scopus and other international indexes. In 2012, the journals from Brazil made up almost 30% of the total number of original and review articles indexed in WoS with a Brazilian affiliation authorship. This represents a proportion much greater than those of South Africa with 16%, China and India with both at 13%, and less than Russia with 53%.

The representation of Brazilian journals in the research output of Brazil indexed in WoS was 17% in 2006, and Brazil ranked 15th in terms of the number of articles. Beginning in 2008, this representation practically doubled as a consequence of the increase of almost 300% in the number of journals indexed, which resulted in Brazil jumping to 13th place in the number of articles indexed. The increase in the number of journals from Brazil indexed in WoS during that period was more than double that of South Africa, China and India, and almost 10 times more than Russia. The contribution of SciELO to these indexes could have been one of the reasons for this marked increase in the indexing of journals from Brazil.

The research that the SciELO journals communicate can be classified as predominantly nationally oriented or of national interest, particularly in the areas of health sciences, agriculture, humanities and social sciences. However, a proportion of the journals, principally in the areas of biology, physical sciences and earth sciences, show an increasing trend towards internationalization. Some indicators give support to this situation.

One indicator is that practically all editors-in-chief and the majority of associate editors are researchers affiliated with institutions from the country that publish the journals. And the Editor-in-Chief is, in general, affiliated to the institution responsible for the journal. In the case of Spanish speaking countries in Latin America, 80% of the articles in the SciELO journals are in Spanish. In the case of Brazil, great efforts are being made to internationalize the journals because of the significant barrier that the Portuguese language represents in communicating with foreign researchers. The percentage of articles in English in Brazilian journals increased from 43% in 2010 to 55% in 2013, while 12% of articles were published simultaneously in Portuguese and English. Along the same lines, the national focus of most of the journals is shown by the predominance of national authors. In the case of Brazil, in the subset of SciELO Brazil journals, only 18% of the articles have a foreign author. Of these, only 6% have Brazilian authors collaborating with foreign authors.

THE WAY FORWARD—PRIORITY ACTION LINES

Certainly, quality journals from developing countries, especially those of the SciELO Network, are relevant to the development of national research, the updating and transference of scientific knowledge for education, professional practices and public policies. They are also important to the development of national capabilities in scholarly editing. And with these capabilities being valued, they should be recognized in the policies and systems of research evaluation.

However, many of the issues that are inherent to carrying out these functions, such as communicating research of limited international interest, often published in languages other than English, or with little international collaboration, achieve, as a whole, limited international impact and place the journals at a competitive disadvantage with international journals of standing in the international indexes which are used as standards in research evaluation systems and policies.

These issues, full of challenges and contradictions, have been part of the evolution of journals in developing countries for a long time.

The SciELO Program, continuing what it has been doing since its inception, will contribute to the enrichment of this evolution, focusing on strengthening the function and purpose of quality journals published nationally, highlighting their relevance in the national and international context of research and scholarly communication.

An alternative index

First and foremost, the SciELO Program will contribute by unequivocally confirming SciELO's character as a selective, multi-disciplinary and multi-lingual bibliographic index, breaking the hegemony of the international indexes, populated for some time by journals from the developed countries with a predominance of journals from commercial publishers, especially the high impact journals.

While being a bibliographic index with full text, SciELO has progressively become recognized as a standard in national research systems, thus contributing, in a qualified way, to broadening the universe of quality journals that are taken into account in research evaluation systems. The principal characteristic of SciELO, as far as being a selective bibliographic index is concerned, is its inclusion in the national education and research systems, which means that it is in a better position to select quality journals and promote their inclusion internationally in comparison with other international indexes. The indexing function of SciELO contributes to the goal of improving quality journals and consequently plays an educational role, together with the publishers and editors, in that capacity. With the inclusion of SciELO CI in the WoS platform, this indexing function of SciELO will be enriched, especially as far as the international inclusion of its journals is concerned.

Adoption of open access

Secondly, the SciELO Program will contribute by unequivocally confirming the adoption of OA as it radically increased the availability and interoperability of the SciELO journals on the Web and of the research they publish, especially after they were indexed in Google and Google Scholar. The ranking of the top portals in the Ranking Web of World Repositories published by the Consejo Superior de Investigaciones Científicas (CSIC) in Spain is used by the SciELO Program as a yardstick to measure the performance of the collections on the Web. In July 2014, among the 157 portals looked at, 7 SciELO collections ranked in the top 20: SciELO Brazil was in 3rd place right behind ResearchGate and Academia.edu; SciELO Chile was 7th; the SciELO.org portal was 9th; SciELO Mexico was 14th; the SciELO Public Health thematic collection was 15th; Spain was 16th and Cuba was 20th. In addition, the performance of the collections and of the journals on the Web is also measured by the number of article downloads which, across the SciELO Network, averages an estimated one million article downloads per day. This network-wide estimate comes from the use of the COUNTER Code of Practice for counting the downloads for just the SciELO Brazil collection over the last two years, which showed a daily average of more than 500,000 downloads. According to Google Analytics, this remarkable performance as measured by downloads is driven by the fact that more than 70% of downloads are from domestic users. This also indicates that the research published by the journals has a predominantly national interest and focus.

Sustainability

Thirdly, in unequivocally confirming SciELO's goal of contributing to the improvement of the indexed journals, the coordinators of the national collections of the SciELO Network, at their meeting held in October 2013 as part of the SciELO 15 Years Conference, approved a set of action lines relating to professionalization, internationalization and financial sustainability to be implemented by the countries over the next three years in line with corresponding national plans[7].

These new action lines will bring about a new phase in the development of the journals of the SciELO Network, in line with the international state of the art, without neglecting SciELO's central focus on national education and research systems. The idea is to provide a common platform of products, services, and processes certified by SciELO for journal management and publishing functions, which will bring about greater efficiencies in the production of the journals.

The development of this platform will include the participation of national and international companies which will compete for the

---

7   SciELO. Action Lines for the Years 2014-2016 with the Objective of Increasing the Visibility of the SciELO Network Journals and Collections (2013)http://www.scielo15.org/wp-content/uploads/2013/10/SciELO-Lineas-de-accion-2014-2016_20131018_EN.pdf

provision of services to the journals. In turn, journal publishers may opt for in-house production with or without the products of the common platform, or combine in-house production with contracting for one or more of the common services, or even outsourcing the operation completely. The objective is, on the one hand, to professionalize the production of the journals and, on the other hand, minimize its impact on the editors-in-chief and associate editors who, keeping in mind the limited time that they can dedicate to journals, should focus on the improvement of the evaluation of manuscripts with the view to improving the quality of the research articles the journals publish. The manuscript review workflow should be supported by online systems that improve the efficiency, transparency and ethics of the processes which involve editors, peer-reviewers and authors.

The common platform will enhance the metapublisher function of SciELO which implies expanding SciELO's role beyond that of indexing and aggregating journals in collections and portals in such a way as to progressively cover all the steps in journal editing, publishing and dissemination. This improvement will be implemented in partnership with the journal publishers and with national and international companies.

The establishment of the platform also aims to minimize the costs of adopting state-of-the-art products and services, and contributing in such a way that support programs for the production of journals and the publishing institutions themselves progressively develop consistent budgets linked to efficient and quality production. To facilitate this process, article charges will be established in order to guide the definition of the production flows and their respective services, as well as joint financing with the support of one or more sources. In particular, this will pave the way for the establishment and operation of an Article Processing Charge (APC) for journals that adopt such a business model. This advance is essential in guiding and supporting the institutions responsible for publishing the journals in OA in a way that demonstrates both quality and sustainability.

Internationality

The development and regular operation of the platform will also contribute to the strengthening of the national and regional capabilities and infrastructures in editing and publishing products, and services in line with international standards.

The implementation of the internationalization action line represents an enormous challenge for the majority of SciELO journals because it requires significant changes in their future design, perception and construction as communication vehicles open nationally and internationally.

This action line envisages breaking and transcending the institutional and geographic insularity of the journals with a broad editorial openness, favoring their inclusion in the international flows of scholarly communication. Many journals were created to provide a place of publication for articles from their respective institutions, geographic regions and subject disciplines which, for one reason or another, are either not suitable or not accepted for publication in foreign journals. Although these reasons may be acceptable, it is also recognized that insularity causes failures, vices and favoritism that opposes efficient scholarly communication.

The indexing criteria of SciELO require transparency in the management and operation of the journals. Based on this, the internationalization action line will foster the expansion of this transparency beyond the borders of the countries in the SciELO Network. Thus, internationalization applies to the make up of the editors and peer-reviewers who must bring in a mixture of national and foreign researchers in their journals along with a progressive increase in authors with foreign affiliations.

Internationalization represents a most difficult barrier to overcome for journals whose scope is essentially national and/or who publish in languages other than English. Constraints of language pose a particularly critical challenge for Brazil given the limited number of Portuguese speaking countries with significant scholarly output. Many Brazilian journals have adopted the path of publishing simultaneously in Portuguese and English as a way to address their different communities of readers. In the case of the other Ibero-American countries, Spanish covers a broad range of countries with significant scholarly production. In any case, the communication of research in English has become mandatory in many subject areas.

The common platform will also contribute to the adoption of innovations already present in international publishing such as: the structuring of full text in XML as the source for generating PDF, EPUB and HTML formats which allow for publishing texts that adjust to the different sizes of computer screens, tablets and smartphones; continuous publishing of articles without needing to wait for the composition of a new issue, and the adoption of social networks for the marketing and dissemination of journals and the research they publish.

The SciELO indexing criteria for the inclusion and retention of journals in the collections will include indicators which will measure the level of professionalization and internationalization that must be progressively adhered to over the next few years in the different subject areas.

Conclusion

In 2013, the SciELO Program celebrated 15 years of uninterrupted operation[8]. This prompted a review of the progress achieved to date, the principal problems and barriers that historically limited the performance of the journals using the classic evaluation methods, and the challenges and the opportunities, in particular, represented by the innovations that are occurring in international scholarly communication. This review concluded with a joint proposal for the promotion and implementation of a new phase in the SciELO Program focusing on the improvement of the journals by means of the professionalization of their editorial management, the internationalization of their working structures and of the authorships of the articles they publish, and in the search for and integration of policies and models of sustainable financing.

The publication of SciELO journals in gold road OA is a well established modus operandi. It will continue to encompass the majority of the quality journals under the SciELO Network. With rare exceptions, national and institutional policies and programs and institutions supporting research and scholarly communication, and institutions responsible for the publication of journals are aligned with the principles that sustain OA to scholarly knowledge and particularly the aspects related to the developing world highlighted in the Salvador Declaration. They are aware of the decisive contribution that OA signifies for increasing the visibility of the research they communicate. However, national research institutions are expected to bring well-defined policies in favor of journals published nationally, particularly towards their sustainable financing.

---

8   SciELO 15 Years (2013) http://www.scielo15.org/en/

The SciELO Program will continue to prioritize the improvement of the journals it indexes by requiring the adoption of advances and innovations in contemporary editing and scholarly publishing, and a positive performance in the evaluations of the management and operation of the journals' editorial and publication processes, principally in the visibility of the published research. The journals and their editors will have the freedom and responsibility to implement and update their editorial policies, manage and operate the evaluation of article submissions, and market and disseminate their programs.

In addition to the improvements in management and operation, the crucial question which affects the evolution of the SciELO Program and, more specifically of the journals it indexes, resides in the understanding and perception by national research systems of the function they exercise in communicating an important portion of national research which is neither suitable nor accepted for publishing in journals of international standing. It is in this context that the SciELO journals can be classified according to their different degrees of national and international focus and, as a consequence, subjected to different levels and scales of evaluation. For example, it makes little or no sense to equate the values of indicators based on the number of citations received by journals that publish in Portuguese or Spanish with the values of journals of international standing that publish in English. Equating different types of journals is absurd and, in general, tends to stigmatize journals published in developing countries as naturally being of low impact. Thus, when national systems of research evaluation use journal citation indicators such as the Impact Factor as a proxy for the impact of their articles, it tends to penalize, a priori, a significant portion of the journals which have a predominantly national focus.

The challenge before us is, therefore, to expand the policies and metrics of evaluation, and adjust their application according to the different levels of national and international focus of journals. These metrics should combine indicators of professionalism in editorial management and quality of the manuscripts review, with indicators of research impact based on the number of citations, downloads and mentions in social networks that the corresponding articles receive.

Overcoming this challenge will be made easier when national research systems go forward with the hoped for abandonment of the use of journals, in particular of the Impact Factor, as a proxy for the quality and impact of research they publish in favor of the use of the individual performance of articles in the context of their respective disciplines.

Online publication, dissemination and indexing systems favor evaluating the visibility and influence of individual articles. In as much as the journal Impact Factor could be abandoned as a proxy for the assessment of research in favor of metrics centered on the performance of individual articles, including citations received, downloads and mentions in social networks by subject area, languages and geographic coverage, the ranking of journals will continue to be important. However, it will no longer be the determining factor in assessing research and will contribute to a more open and competitive environment for journals in the process of attracting article submissions of increasing quality. This "emancipation" will favor publication in OA, and in particular the SciELO Program and its journals.

Bibliographic References

Cetto, AM & Alonso-Gamboa, O 1998, 'Scientific periodicals in Latin America and the Caribbean: a global perspective', *Interciencia*, no. 23, pp. 84-93.

Krzyzanowski, RF & Ferreira, MCG 1998, 'Avaliação de periódicos científicos e técnicos brasileiros', *Ciência da Informação*, vol. 27, no. 2.

Krzyzanowski, RF et al. 1991, 'Programa de apoio às revistas científicas para a FAPESP', *Ciência da Informação*, vol. 20, no. 2, pp. 137-150.

Miguel, S et al. 2011, 'Open access and Scopus: a new approach to scientific visibility from the standpoint of access', *Journal of the American Society for Information Science and Technology*, vol. 62, no. 6, pp. 1130-1145.

Meneghini, R 1998, 'Avaliação da produção científica e o Projeto SciELO', *Ciência da Informação*, vol. 27, no. 2, pp. 219-220.

Packer, AL 2010, 'The SciELO open acess: a gold way from the south', *Canadian Journal of Higher Education*, vol. 39, no. 3, pp. 111-126.

Packer, AL 2014, 'The emergence of journals of Brazil and scenarios for their future', *Educação e Pesquisa*, vol. 40, no. 2, pp. 301-323.

Packer, AL & Castro, E (eds) 2008, *Virtual health library*, BIREME/PAHO/WHO, São Paulo.

Packer, AL et al. 2014, *SciELO – 15 years of open access: an analytic study of open access and scholarly communication*, UNESCO, Paris.

Prat, AM 2000, 'Programa Biblioteca Científica Eletrónica em Línea, SciELO-Chile, una nueva forma de acceder a la literatura científica nacional', *Biological Research*, vol. 33, no. 2, p. 9.

Ribeiro, CK et al. 2007, 'Construção de modelo-síntese para análise de periódicos científicos' in *Encontro Nacional de Pesquisa em Ciëncia da Informação* no. 8.

Souza, EP & Paula, MCS 2002, 'QUALIS: a base de qualificação dos periódicos científicos utilizada na avaliação CAPES', *Infocapes*, vol. 10, no. 2, pp. 7-25.

All websites accessed between August and September 2014.

Facts & Figures:
Russian Federation

Country and Economy

Capital	Name of Capital: Moscow
Area	In km²: 17,075,157
Population Size	2013 Estimate: 142,833,689 Country Ranking: 9
Density	Per km²: 8
GDP (nominal)	In Billions of US$ (2014 estimate): 2,677,542 Country Ranking: 6
GDP per Capita	In US$ (2014 estimate): 18,995 Country Ranking: 46
Human Development Index	HDI (2012): 0.788 Country Ranking: 55

Research and Open Access

Scientists	Total Number (2009) (in thousand): 442.3 Per Capita: 3,091 per 1 million
Expenditures on Research and Development	In Billions of US$ (2011): 23.8 % of GDP: 1% Country Ranking: 10
Publications	Total Number (2013): 43,930 Country Ranking: 15 Number of Citable Documents: 42,512
Citations	Total Number (2013): 13,057 Country Ranking: 22 Citations per Document: 0.3 H-Index: 355
Journals	Total Number of Academic and Scholarly Journals (2014): 1,869 Journals with Impact Factor (2012): 142
Open Archives	Institutional Repositories: 20 Disciplinary Repositories: 1 Aggregating Repositories: 0 Governmental Repositories: 1
Open Access Journals	Total Number of Open Access Journals • UlrichsWeb: 157 • DOAJ: 97

OVERVIEW

Open access to scientific and technical information in Russia is at the very early phases of its progress. The development of the international open access movement in the late 90s and early 2000s coincides with hard times for Russian science. The negative impact of unsuccessful reforms and economic crises in Russia overrun the effect of discontent caused by the growth of journal subscription costs. Amidst other reasons one could mention the weakness of civil society responsibility, which was rather typical for Russian scholars. Poor knowledge of English also plays a negative role, as this language became the main language of international scientific communication. Only a few Russian repositories are registered by the OpenDOAR directory. Another example: 2012 usage statistics from the international ArXiv repository for e-prints 200 does not mention any Russian university or research institution among the 200 heaviest user institutions.

However, there are several positive open access projects by the Russian government, the Academy of Sciences, by universities, information centres and engaged scientists and information professionals. The following chapter will address the landscape of these projects, distinguishing between published and unpublished (grey) scientific literature. "Published" means here above all commercial, scientific and technical information, mostly books and journals, while "grey literature" stands for theses and dissertations, R&D reports and so on, mainly produced by public research organizations and higher education, without commercial purpose.

The impact of history and society is obvious, perhaps more than in other countries. The Russian Federation is the largest country in the world, both in Europe and in Asia, and it is heir to the empire of the Tsars and the superpower of the USSR. In the Russian context, open access signifies more than Internet and scientific communication: it is public-funded free dissemination of research results to society, in the socialist tradition of common good and public interest. Also, public institutions and authorities play a substantial role in the open access movement, prevailing over individual initiatives. The authors, both with longstanding experience in the production and dissemination of scientific information since the late Soviet Union, raise three interesting questions:
1. The early open access movement made a kind of amalgam between open access, open science and open society, in the American way

of understanding. In other words, they linked efficient and direct scientific communication to a specific form of social and political development. Is this true for the Russian open access movement?

2. There is an on-going discussion in the open access movement on business models and financial aspects, beyond the terms of "free", "libre" and "gratis". Someone has to pay, but who should or will? This paper does not leave any doubt: the dissemination of public research and access to scientific information, *a fortiori* open access, is part of the State's responsibility and must be supported and organized by the government and regional or local authorities. In other countries, open access is increasingly supported by the corporate sector, via funding agencies and commercial publishers. Which is the best way to assure sustainability?

3. Last particularity: regarding law and copyright, the open access movement often opposes public v. publishers' interests, considering the scientific authors as potential allies. Here, the potential conflict is clearly elsewhere, between the authors' rights of intellectual property and the public's interest and right to information. In other words, the authors (at least those delegating their interests to commercial publishers) are considered as a potential problem in the way of open access.

The chapter finally raises another question, on the meaning of open access to scientific results. The OA movement defines it as free and unrestricted access to documents and data files on the Internet. In the following contribution, the meaning appears to be larger, including free access to research tools, facilities, print documents, catalogue records and metadata, abstracts, databases and translations. The authors define OA as a continuum of services and dissemination channels, also as a historical and societal continuum from print to digital resources.

About the Authors

Andrey I. Zemskov graduated from the Moscow Institute of Technical Physics (State University), as an engineer-physicist on experimental nuclear physics. He obtained his PhD on plasma physics at the Kurchatov Institute of Atomic Energy, Moscow. From 1990 to 2006 he was the Director of the Russian National Public Library for Science and Technology (NPLS&T), since 2006 he is the Director Advisor of the same library. He has published four monographs and more than 70 papers on librarianship, grey literature, electronic resources, copyright, ecology, etc. His research interests are library management, library statistics, grey literature, electronic resources, copyright issues, information ecology.

Leonid P. Pavlov graduated from the Moscow Physical-Engineering Institute (now National Nuclear Research University), Dipl. Eng. in computer systems. He holds a PhD in informatics. He is working at the Centre of Information Technologies and Systems for Executive Power Authorities (CIT&S). He participated in the R&D, implementation and management of nation-wide information systems for grey literature as Scientific Researcher, Project Manager, Acting Director, Specialist-in-Chief. He is the author of more than 100 scholarly works in Russian and English. His main fields of scientific interest are grey literature and information systems.

Open Access in Russia: The Beginning of a Long Way

Andrey I. Zemskov and Leonid P. Pavlov

> Tornate all'antico e sarà un progresso
> Giuseppe Verdi[1]

Back in the USSR

Past experience is useful to better understand the present and forecast the future. Paradoxically, the problem of providing free open access (OA) to scientific and technical information (STI) was successfully solved in the Soviet Union, bearing in mind, of course, that it was pre-Internet OA. To the question "who is to pay?" the socialist economy decided on the only answer, "the state". And the Soviet state did fund science and OA to research results in particular. In accordance with the planned economy the 100% state funding of science was regular and stable on the level of about 3.5% of the gross domestic product (GDP). After the end of the Soviet Union, science funding dropped to only 0.3% in 1996 and today represents approximately 1.5% of the GDP.

The State System for Scientific and Technical Information (abbreviated in Russian as GSNTI) served as a reliable legal, financial and organizational framework for the sphere of STI in the USSR. Government decisions that had the force of law secured the status and

---

1   "Let us turn to the past: that will be progress"–Letter to Francesco Florimo, January 5, 1871, cited from Francesco Florimo *Riccardo Wagner ed i wagneristi* (Ancona: A. G. Morelli, 1883) p.108; translation from Charles Osborne (ed. and trans.) *Letters of Giuseppe Verdi* (London: Victor Gollancz, 1971) p. 169.

funding of the system. GSNTI included a hierarchy of information institutions with a number of federal-level centers, each responsible for a particular type of scientific and technical information document, e.g. papers from scientific journals, patents, books, serial publications etc. Beside the central institutions there were local STI centers in every regional capital and thousands of STI departments in scientific institutions, universities and large enterprises.

OA is supported by an ethical argument that if scientific research is funded by the taxpayers they are supposed to have free access to research results (Jeffery 2006). The socialist solution to the old conflict between the author and public interests was entirely in favor of the public that was granted free access to the fruit of the author's research even if sometimes the system infringed upon the author's interests. The annual budget was sufficient to collect the STI resources using the legal deposit mechanisms and to disseminate the information in different ways and always for free to the public. Not only the reading rooms and collections of libraries and information centers and interlibrary loans but also all kinds of subscriptions to peer-reviewed and abstract journals, document copy delivery and other information services like selective dissemination of information were free for users and paid by the state-funded institutions and organizations the users belonged to. Thus, a real pre-Internet OA was realized.

The disintegration of the Soviet Union and the change from a socialist to a market economy in the Russian Federation urged the transformation of political and economic paradigms that in practice turned out to be much more painful and less successful than in theory. The post-Soviet transformation, characterized by political unrest and general disorder badly affected the economy and science. However, the economic efficiency of science emerged on the government agenda again for the following reasons. First, the budget for scientific research and development decreased dramatically so there was an urgent need for allocating and distributing the "scientific" money most effectively. Second, an overwhelming majority of scientific research and development was (in the Soviet Union) and still is (in Russia) state-funded. A decade or so ago and even up till now about 70% of financial support for science still comes from the state while Russian private business is reluctant to invest in scientific research.

This factor is important in order to understand why the Russian state plays a different role in scientific results and intellectual property production and rights distribution compared to Western countries. Because of this difference the direct implementation of the experience and legislation on intellectual property borrowed from abroad, say, from the USA or Europe should be done with great care and in any case with deep understanding of the Russian specificity. If the Soviet approach was completely in favor of public interests, the new Russian Copyright Law supports the author's interest much more to the detriment of OA and public interests. Yet, since the Russian State and business prefer to import products and technologies rather than invest in the fruit of domestic science, nobody really converts new knowledge into money.

Our paper will provide a short overview on OA in the Russian Federation, then focus on grey literature and published documents and, after some comments on the legal situation, conclude with two aspects, that is, public funding and the language barrier.

Empirical elements

Open access to scientific and technical information in Russia is at the very early stages of its progress. The development of the OA movement and organizations at the end of the 1990s and early 2000s (1997 SPARC coalition, 2001 Creative Commons, 2003 Berlin Declaration, etc.) coincided with hard times for Russian science. The negative impact of unsuccessful reforms and economic crises in Russia outweigh the effect of discontentment caused by the growth of journal subscription costs that disturbed the world's librarians.

Amidst other reasons one could mention the weakness of civil society responsibility, which was rather typical for Russian professional communities of scholars. People preferred to obtain immediate remuneration for their research with no attention to predicting the consequences.

Poor knowledge of English also plays a negative role, despite the fact that this language has become an international language in scientific communication. OA archives contain a lot of documents in English. According to the OpenDOAR directory of open repositories, there are 44 Russian language archives (13th position in ranking) whereas 1,762 English language archives hold first position in language rankings. Very indicative of this is the low usage of OA ArXiv system, which provides access to scientific e-prints. ArXiv statistics for the calendar year of 2012 presenting 200 of the heaviest user institutions does not show any Russian university or research institution address.

With the English language situation in mind an important role of the All-Russian Institute for Scientific and Technical Information (VINITI) in support of OA to foreign scientific literature should be admitted. VINITI performs the abstracting in Russian of the world STI flow, mainly in English, and publishes 207 abstract journals on all branches of science and technology. Unfortunately, the abstracting and issuing of the journals take approximately one year for Russian sources and 1.5 to 2 years for foreign language publications. Still, there are several other positive examples of OA activity by the Russian government, Academies of Sciences, universities, information centers and enthusiasts in respect to both published and non-published (grey) literature.

The heritage of history: from grey literature to open access

The traditional advantages of grey literature, that is, valuable content and fast availability, are amplified today by the fact that it has become the main information source of the virtual network reality just as printed matter played the main role in human communications from the 15th and up to the end of the 20th century. A well-known definition of grey literature was given at the 6th International Conference on Grey Literature in New York City in 2004: "Information produced on all levels of government, academics, business and industry in electronic and print formats not controlled by commercial publishing, that is, where publishing is not the primary activity" (Schöpfel & Farace 2010).

Also, the most important and distinctive attribute of grey literature is its non-commercial or non-profit production and distribution, which fits in with the network environment of open source and open archives where the non-commercial paradigm prevails. The function of scientists (and of grey literature as their information support) is to convert money into knowledge, not vice versa. Another important aspect of grey literature is that it is "literature" and nothing else; so all the trash like bus schedules, flyers, receipts etc. should be considered as ephemera and not as grey literature.

Russian specificities

Three remarks should be made about the Russian specificity in this domain.

First, while in some countries the two terms "thesis" and "dissertation" may have different meanings, in Russia they are synonyms and apply only to post-graduate works. In fact, the term "dissertation" («диссертация» in Cyrillic) has been applied only to two kinds of post-graduate work; to the so-called candidate and doctoral dissertations. "Candidate of Sciences" can be compared to the PhD in the USA, whereas "Doctor of Sciences" is superior to "Candidate of Sciences" and seems to have no direct analogue in the Western world where the title "Dr" may be applied either to PhD or just to a university graduate. As a rule, in Russia one cannot become a Doctor without being a Candidate. Until recently when Russia joined the Bologna Process in higher education the word "dissertation" had never been used for graduate work which was called "Diploma work" or (for engineering sciences) "Diploma project" or, in general, "graduate qualification work".

Secondly, there is a difference between the English and the Russian meaning of "science". The Russian «наука» is broader and includes not only exact, natural and engineering sciences but also humanities, arts, social sciences, law and medicine.

Thirdly, a reiterated skepticism about the credibility of grey literature is based on the assertion that it is not peer-reviewed. However, at least in Russia the most valuable types of grey literature – scientific and technical reports and candidate and doctoral theses – are not less reliable than published literature because of a centralized system for the collection, processing and archiving of these documents, established fifty years ago and supported by the Centre for Information Technologies and Systems (CITIS, formerly VNTIC). Based on federal law and governmental decisions, the CITIS collections contain today more than seven million items, either in full-text or in abstract (Starovoitov et al. 2012).

Infrastructure and digital resources

Without organized acquisition, digital storing and accessing technologies there is no OA to grey literature. In the field of grey literature, the leading agency of the State System for Scientific and Technical Information (GSNTI) was the Scientific and Technical Information Centre of Russia (abbreviated in Russian as VNTIC, now merged with CITIS). The status and activities profile of VNTIC was (and of CITIS is) similar to that of the National Technical

Information Service (NTIS) in the United States with the difference that the Russian centre is responsible not only for scientific and technical reports but also for dissertations (Pavlov 2002).

The grey literature information system has been operating since 1975. It was created as the grey literature section of the national library-information fund of the USSR and part of the GSNTI. The system consisted of two divisions: the full-text R&D reports and dissertations (the so-called primary documents) stored on microfiches and the bibliographic cards with abstracts (the so-called secondary documents) stored on the mainframe computer in a database format. There were two kinds of secondary documents: "registration cards" for new R&D projects and "information cards" for reports and dissertations (Pavlov 1998). In the early eighties the grey literature system became the host core of the computer network called AIST (abbreviated in Russian for "computerized teleprocessing information network"). AIST connected distant smart terminals, a prototype of personal computers situated all over the country, to the host-computer with the grey literature databases situated in Moscow. The network operated in a dial-up mode through the switched public telephone lines, with more than 500 transactions per day (information search and retrieval, copy-ordering). That was the first IT network of the pre-Internet era in the country and paved the way for the OA network to grey literature. No matter how obsolete its soft- and hardware may seem today – this system met from the very beginning all the major requirements for a centralized digital library, and for several decades, its basic configuration survived through technological changes from mainframe computers to PCs, database and network servers and information migrating from magnetic tapes and microfiches through diskettes and CDs to the modern digital data stores.

As in the past, the actual federal STI system for grey literature covers the whole range of scientific research and development activities, that is, all disciplines, and the whole territory of the Russian Federation. The system is hosted on the CITIS technological platform. In 2004, it was included by decree of the President of the Russian Federation, in the list of strategically important systems. Since 2010 it has been listed in the Federal Register of the State Information Systems.

The acquisition of full-text reports and dissertations is based on legal deposit principles in accordance with the Federal Law "On the obligatory copy of documents". The law obliges all organizations (collective authors of reports) and persons (individual authors of dissertations) to deposit a free full-text copy at the CITIS. In return, the CITIS must develop (complete) the collection, permanently store (archive) the documents and disseminate information on new content. The disciplinary structure of the report and dissertation collections is shown in table 2.1.

	REPORTS	DISSERTATIONS
Engineering and applied sciences	84.6%	56.6%
Social sciences and humanities	13.9%	15.9%
Natural and exact sciences	11.6%	28.6%
Others, interdisciplinary	6.7%	3.3%

Table 2.1: Disciplinary structure of the CITIS report and dissertation holdings

The CITIS collection consists of full-text primary documents and related metadata. Until 2004 for dissertations and 2006 for reports, the documents were stored on microfiches. Since then, incoming print documents are scanned and stored both in TIFF and PDF format in a full-text digital repository. Their metadata (secondary documents) contain detailed bibliographic descriptions (more than 30 different data) and abstracts and are stored in a structured database for information search and retrieval. From 1982 to 2010 these metadata had been keyed in by the CITIS. From 2010 on, the authors themselves have to enter the metadata into the system via an online interface. In the future, a new system will allow online submission of digital reports and dissertations, with authentication by electronic signature. Each document has a unique inventory number (identifier) both in the database (metadata record) and in the repository (full-text). Table 2.2 provides some figures about the CITIS resources (December 2013).

	REPORTS	DISSERTATIONS
Records with abstracts	1,300,000	700,000
Documents	830,000	700,000
Digital files	85,000	280,000

Table 2.2: Content of CITIS database and repository (since 1984)

Along with the reports from more than 14,000 organizations, the CITIS database contains detailed information about nearly 1.3 million R&D projects. A small part of the metadata records – 80,000 – have been translated into English. Older documents on microfiche are scanned and converted into PDF files on request. Table 2.3 below shows the development of the CITIS database and holdings, from 2000 to 2012 (Starovoitov et al. 2014).

	Projects (records)	Reports (records)	Reports (full-text)	Dissertations
2000	13,879	11,101	6,400	24,453
2004	13,000	10,800	6,500	25,460
2008	14,982	10,536	6,899	25,226
2010	21,100	15,300	11,000	24,700
2011	31,000	19,600	14,500	24,780
2012	32,798	19,860	14,360	24,200

Table 2.3: The development of the CITIS database and holdings (2000-2012)

The figures show how the overall number of CITIS resources continuously increased from 2000 to 2012: the annual input of registered R&D project increased by 236%, of report metadata by 179% and of full-text reports by 224%. Only the annual number of dissertations remained stable, at roughly 25,000 dissertations per year (as many as in the Soviet Union), with 15% doctoral dissertations.

The users of the CITIS system are able to conduct online subject search via the Internet only in the database. This means that so far only secondary documents (metadata records) are really OA. Additionally, the CITIS publishes both digital and print abstract journals with information about registered projects, reports and dissertations in 25 subject series. For full-text documents, due to legal reasons OA is limited to the premises of the CITIS reading room (Intranet). Most individual users are researchers, experts, lecturers and tutors, under- and post-graduate students. Among collective users are different kinds of organizations – scientific research institutes, universities, industrial and business community, state executive and controlling authorities (ministries, agencies, audit and fiscal bodies, law-courts). Official users usually require statistical, financial and general information on science.

The Federal grey literature system contains more and more digital content, and the centralized system architecture provides positive solutions to several problems typical for online repositories: a well-organized legal deposit with a complete digital collection of full-text reports and dissertations; a unified system of documents registration, bibliographic control, indexing, search and retrieval; a user-friendly "one window" access to all the Russian reports and dissertations at one place and on one URL address; a secured and reliable permanent storage and archiving of the information resources for future generations. Technologically there is no obstacle for the system to become fully OA, and the free dissemination of grey literature metadata with abstracts is a first step[2]. In fact, the problems with full OA are not technological but legal and financial (see below).

OA TO PUBLISHED INFORMATION SOURCES

The Russian Academy of Sciences (RAS)

So far there is no comprehensive OA program of the Russian Academy of Sciences (RAS). Nevertheless several limited projects are underway, such as the Electronic Research Library (e-Library), created by the Russian Foundation for Basic Research (RFBR), an affiliated body of the RAS. Other initiatives were taken in the field of social sciences and by the Siberian department. Some collections similar to open archives have been launched in the framework of the RAS "scientific heritage" program, which consists of electronic files of biographies and proceedings of prominent Russian scientists[3].

e-Library

Strictly speaking, e-Library is not an OA system. It is rather a multidisciplinary scientific library with open registration. But it serves the scientific community without financial or legal access barriers.

E-Library was established in 1999 as a joint project of the RFBR and the academic publisher Springer Verlag. It provides OA to about 18

---

2   See the portal at http://www.citis.rntd.ru

3   http://e-heritage.ru

million bibliographic records and abstracts of research articles. One does not need any subscription or registration, except for the abstract journal in which abstracts are licensed items. Besides, more than 2,400 scientific journals are using the e-Library platform to post OA full text articles (table 2.4). To access the full text one has to be a registered library user.

Journal titles, total	46,508
of which Russian journals	8,645
Full text journals, total	7,776
of which Russian journals	3,320
of which OA journals	2,914
Total number of issues	11,911,497
Total number of articles	18,702,984
Total number of cited references	143,065,226
Registered users	984,023

Table 2.4: Statistics of e-Library (accessed March 11, 2014)

Moreover, based on the recorded articles and cited references, e-Library provides the data for the Russian Science Citation Index. In essence this library is using the nation-wide licensing system, with license cost covered by the RFBR and the Ministry of Education and Science of the Russian Federation.

Social Sciences

The OA program of the RAS department of social sciences is supported by grants from the Ford Foundation for the development of the Socionet system, by EU grants for the development of online infrastructure as well as via the RAS computerization program. The goal of the program is to build a corpus of OA publications on current research in social sciences freely available on the Internet. This new service will include shared workspace, networking tools, links to cited documents and usage data for scientists and institutions.

In 2007 the Central Economics and Mathematics Institute (CEMI) of the Russian Academy of Sciences, Moscow, joined the international initiative "OA to research results" (Parinov et al. 2013). Compliant with the Berlin Declaration the CEMI created an institutional repository and decided on a mandatory policy, which urges the scientists to deposit their research reports in the repository. CEMI will exploit the usage statistics of the deposits and the evaluation and salary bonuses of individual researchers.

The CEMI repository content includes all scientific production of CEMI researchers and is freely available online. The extended bibliographic records (metadata) with links to full text are freely available for use in subject collections, search systems, and other information resources.

All research papers, including those supported by the scientific grant systems, should be published in peer-reviewed publications or (if it is not done six months after the project) deposited in the institutional repository as pre-print. After acceptance for publication, the author's version should be deposited in an institutional archive as an electronic post-print. If the publisher requires exclusive rights, the author is recommended to deposit the metadata with a notice on availability of the paper on demand via the author's e-mail address (for instance in the "document status" field).

The repository combines subject collections and unique documents and is connected, via an OAI-PMH interface to international archives and aggregating services; also, it is registered by ROAR and other national and international directories.

Older materials and research results should also be part of the institutional archive. Ideally, CEMI researchers would disseminate 100% of their scientific output in OA, thus providing an exhaustive presentation of scientific activity. All divisions of CEMI need to appoint a person responsible for electronic deposit in the institutional archive. He should be well trained and able to manage collections of relevant divisions and to consult division personnel on self-archiving procedures. This person will create subject collections inside the personal areas of Socionet and will post research material. The system administrator adds these collections to the institutional profile. Establishing links between the personal collections and the CEMI profile means the inclusion of these collections into the institutional open archive.

The procedure of self-deposit takes 2-3 minutes if the bibliographic record and the full text files are ready. Before the first self-deposit, the author must create his/her personal area in Socionet. The compilation of all usage statistics related to his/her works should be linked to the personal profile.

Along with the CEMI, twenty other RAS institutions have created institutional repositories, such as the Institute of Philosophy, the Institute of Economic Forecasting and the Institute of Economics (all in Moscow) or the Institute of Socio-Economic Development of Territories (Vologda). The institutional repository of the Market Economy Institute (MEI) in Moscow for instance contains several types of scientific output, like monographs, reports, articles, dissertation abstracts, personal data, unpublished papers or MEI news.

Furthermore, the CEMI OA policy integrates active participation in national and international projects and initiatives. CEMI is a member of the international professional association euroCRIS, which supports the development of formats and tools of current research information systems (CRIS) and their integration into national online infrastructure for research institutions and scholars (research e-infrastructure). CEMI's participation in the "European Research Area" program stimulates improvement of organizational and behavioral models of Russian research institutions and scholars. The most important tasks include implementation of the electronic articles and reports submission system followed by professional accreditation and promotion of bonus practice in the RAS institutions.

Since August 2012 the largest international OA electronic library on Economics RePEc.org accepts Russian language collections provided by Socionet. Up to now, RePEc contains three Russian collections, that is, *Voprosy ekonomiki* (Problems of economics), *Nauchnye otchety Instituta problem rynka* (Scientific reports of the MEI) and *Monografii sotrudnikov IPR RAN* (monographs of MEI researchers).

The Siberian Section of the Russian Academy of Sciences

In Siberia, the Russian Academy of Sciences conducted two different OA initiatives, one gold and the other green.

Gold: in 2004 the Sobolev Institute of Mathematics launched the annual digital OA journal *Siberian Electronic Mathematical Reports*. The objective is the rapid electronic dissemination of scientific papers on all subjects of mathematics (differential equations, dynamic systems, mathematical physics, geometry and topology, computational mathematics and so on), of short communications, institutional news and book reviews. All articles are peer-reviewed. The journal is refereed and indexed by Mathematical Reviews, Math-Net.Ru, eLibrary.ru (Russian Science Citation Index), and Scopus.

Green: the Institute of Economics and Industrial Engineering (IEIE) at Novosibirsk launched an open institutional repository for their publications. The platform provides access to dissertations, proceedings and scientific reports from the different IEIE departments, together with monographs, textbooks and journals like *Region: Economics and Sociology*. In addition, it contains the catalogue of IEIE publications, institutional news and organization profiles, pre-prints and other publications of IEIE researchers on regional issues since 1990, and in particular publications by Grigorij Kharin (born 1937), professor in economy at the Novosibirsk State Technical University and author of several monographs on the economy of the USSR and Russia.

The Ministry of Science and Education

The activity of the Ministry of Science and Education of the Russian Federation covers high and higher schools and the Russian National Public Library for Science and Technology (NPLS&T).

Educational resources

Launched in 2002, the Russian high school portal[4] has been continuously growing in the number of services and volume of presented resources. Another portal "United Collection of Digital Educational Resources"[5] has been providing OA to more than 110,000 documents and other learning materials for continuous education and qualification since 2006. The portal is part of the National Foundation on Personnel Training, a non-commercial organization supported with a $68 million grant by the International Bank of Reconstruction and Development.

The "Single window for access to educational resources"[6] is one of the best-known Russian educational sites with 70–80,000 visitors and 150-200,000 searches per working day, mostly from Russia (75–85%)

---

4   http://www.school.edu.ru

5   http://www.school-collection.edu.ru

6   http://window.edu.ru

but also from Ukraine (8–12%), Belorussia (3–5%) and Kazakhstan (3–4%). It aggregates more than 55,000 resources from several regions, universities and research institutions, such as courseware, scientific papers, links to other sites, methods for teachers and students and also for scientists and education managers. The content is indexed by Google, Yandex, Rambler and other search engines.

Towards a mandatory policy

The Ministry of Science and Education is preparing a directive for all higher education institutions to post the qualifying works and dissertations of undergraduate and graduate students on institutional repositories. The governmental Strategic Initiative Agency and the private Yandex Company support the directive and are helping to formulate technical requirements for search engine optimization. The goal is to eliminate plagiarism and to facilitate students' recruitment. The implementation of this directive will be a condition for the accreditation of higher education institutions.

Some public institutions have already implemented such a mandatory policy. For instance, the Saint Petersburg State University requires from all departments and faculties OA to dissertations and theses. Several faculties like the Higher School of Management and Sociology are publishing students' works in English. The department of Mathematics and Mechanics, System Programming, disseminates defending discussion video material in OA along with dissertations. Some faculties permit embargo periods up to one year while others prefer immediate publication. Together with the State University, other Saint Petersburg higher education institutions have started to experiment with open repositories and OA policies, such as the universities of Culture and Arts, Engineering Economics and Exact Mechanics and Technics or the Polytechnic Institute.

Two case studies

The academic library of the Gorky Ural State University at Yekaterinburg created a digital open archive[7] with DSpace software, with more than 600 digitized items and several thousand pages – PhD dissertations, course material, journals, older books and other collections from different faculties and disciplines (literature,

---

7   http://elar.usu.ru

philosophy, journalism, biology). Some projects required specific agreements with rights-holders, others involved partnerships with other institutions, such as a collection of learning material in philosophy (15,000 pages) from the Udmurt State University. 94% of these items are in English, and most of them – 73% – are freely available on the Internet in OA. The other documents can be accessed via the university network (16%) or only at the library (11%). The librarians explain the successful development of their open repository through an active acquisition policy, including the newest conference proceedings, by the use of permanent identifiers and the significant percentage of English language items.

Another successful example of an OA initiative is run by the Chemistry Department of the Lomonosov State University in Moscow. The "Electronic Library on Chemistry" was created in 1994 as a thematic repository on ChemNet.ru, which is the most visited site on chemistry in Russia. All six Russian centers of chemical information[8] contribute to this digital library, with several different types of documents, both published and unpublished:

- Full-text educational materials:
    - materials for high school courses on chemistry, training problems for entrants, electronic textbooks, problems for Olympiads on chemistry;
    - multimedia publications: video lectures, "Basics of Nanotechnology", "General and Inorganic Chemistry", labs, 3D models, etc.;
    - materials for undergraduate students: handbooks, textbooks, lectures, computer programs, databases
- Selected reviews
- Educational methodic materials
- Electronic versions of journals ("Moscow University Chemistry Bulletin", free electronic version since 1998, "Russian Chemistry

---

[8] Chemistry Department of the Lomonosov State University (Moscow), Boreskov Institute of Catalysis (Novosibirsk), Institute of Physics (Saint Petersburg), RAS Photochemistry Centre (Moscow), RAS Institute for High Energy Density (Moscow), RAS Zelinsky Institute of Organic Chemistry (Moscow).

Journal", free electronic version since 2000, "Membranes", free electronic version since 2000)

Bibliographic databases, for example the online database of thermodynamic constants, and a catalogue of Internet resources complete this rich content.

The success of this repository can also be measured in terms of international visibility: depending on the different collections, one third (*Russian Chemistry Journal*) to one half (*Moscow University Chemistry Bulletin*) of the visitors are from abroad, outside of the Russian Federation.

The Russian National Public Library for Science and Technology

For several years the Russian National Public Library for Science and Technology (NPLS&T) disseminated the free library UNESCO software CDS-ISIS to Russian libraries. Later, NPLS&T supplied the proprietary integrated library system IRBIS to several Russian libraries, including the Russian Orthodox Church libraries. The highly ranked NPLS&T website provides OA to different full text collections, like the *SciTech libraries* journal archive, proceedings from NPLS&T, Crimea and LIBNET conferences, NPLS&T annual reports and news and so on.

NPLS&T also developed a special course for undergraduates and librarians on intellectual property rights applied to electronic documents and Internet technologies. Through its participation in the IFLA Committee on Copyright and other Legal Matters and special training sessions NPLS&T actively promotes OA principles amidst Russian librarians.

Ecology and OA

Ecology and OA have in common the principle of social responsibility. Ecology is close to the interests of the general public, and without public involvement and support all efforts will be in vain. OA facilitates public awareness and communication of scientific results. The Directory of OA Journals (DOAJ) contains nearly 200 journals and more than 6,500 articles on ecology, most of them in English and only 14 in Russian.

The OA journal *Printsipy Ekologii* (Ecology Principles) is published by the Petrozavodsk State University (Karelia, Russian Federation). All papers are free of charge both for authors and customers. Everybody can read, download, copy, disseminate and print the content of the journal without the permission of the author or the publisher.

Following recommendations from the President of the Russian Federation, the Fedorov Institute of Applied Geophysics (Moscow) created an OA portal with data and other material on the Earth's ionosphere. Since 2011 the digital scientific journal *Heliogeophysical research* has started to publish the "Proceedings of Fedorov Institute of Applied Geophysics" on the physics of the atmosphere and hydrosphere, environmental control, mathematical modeling and other related topics. All papers in *Heliogeophysical research* are free of charge both for authors and customers.

The same situation exists for another journal, the *Geospace Bulletin*[9] with papers on space physics and physics of the atmosphere. Both journals on ecology have non-profit business models and are completely free, without subscription costs or article processing charges.

Legal aspects

The latest version of the Copyright Law (January 1, 2008) is included in Part IV of the Civil Code of the Russian Federation. This version came out as a result of a heated discussion in the press and within the scientific community on intellectual property of scientific results. Roughly speaking there were two different groups of experts: those claiming the priority of the state and public interests and those holding on to the primacy of the personal (author's) interests. Though there was no unanimous opinion on the question the latter attitude prevailed in the Law thus creating serious obstacles for OA to STI in Russia. Since the problems of the new law became evident, experts and law-makers are now working on a next version of Part IV with the objective to secure public interests.

The dissemination of abstracts and bibliographic information on reports and dissertations in print or digital format is compliant with the law. But with regards to reports, dissertations or other publications, the law requires that any presentation or reproduction needs the author's consent. Getting permission from and/or

---

9   http://vestnik.geospace.ru

concluding agreement with tens of thousands of authors of reports, dissertations etc., is impracticable. However, the law allows for very limited OA to them, via Intranet in local reading rooms and without printing or downloading facilities. Also, readers can order print copies but only of parts and not of complete reports or dissertations. There is no legal norm of how "long" this "short fragment" may be but *de facto* it is agreed that it must not exceed one printer's sheet (24 standard A4 pages). Since CITIS is the only holder of the unique federal collection of Russian scientific and technical reports and except for some institutional repositories with OA to a selection of their own reports, up to now the only place to get free access to the whole collection of full-text reports in digital format is the CITIS reading room.

Recently, two new developments have supported OA, especially to dissertations. The first way is the so-called virtual reading rooms of the resource holders. The point is that Part IV of the Civil Code, as we mentioned above, permits that the digital full texts of dissertations may be available to readers on the screens of monitors at the collection holder's reading room with no means of either paper printout or electronic download. So, to provide a wider OA and keep within the law, besides the main reading room at the collection holder's premises, it is possible to organize virtual reading rooms in other scientific and/or university structures all over Russia allowing distant users to have access to digital dissertations through the Internet. The visitors of the virtual reading rooms are subjected to the same copyright limitations as the main reading room visitors: they must be registered as distant readers of the main reading room and are allowed to read the texts only from within the precincts of the distant reading room. Now this approach has been successfully introduced into practical use by the Russian State Library, the main library of the Russian Federation and the second (after CITIS) holder of the complete collection of the Russian dissertations acquired from CITIS in digital form. The Library has created more than 550 virtual reading rooms in many cities and higher school institutions all over Russia and abroad. The potential audience of the reading rooms is estimated at one million scholars. It is evident that the longer the distance of the reading room from Moscow the more its services are demanded.

The second solution has become feasible with the Russian Federation Government Decision No 842 of September 24, 2013 "On the regulations of scientific degrees conferment". This new decision introduces the public online notification system that makes it obligatory for the Candidates and Doctors of science to deposit their digital dissertation on the Internet site or repository of the organization where the official public defence of the dissertation is to take place. For the Candidate's degree the full-text dissertations must be in OA no less than two months before and seven months after the official defence; for the Doctor's degree the terms are three and nine months. So, the 2013 decision establishes mandatory free OA to digital dissertations for nine months (Candidate dissertations) and twelve months (Doctoral dissertations). The objective is to improve the scientific standard of dissertations by public discussion and to avoid plagiarism via public OA, even if this OA is limited in time and looks like a kind of "inverted embargo". Also, since the dissertations are submitted by their author and with his/her consent, there is no conflict with the Copyright Law.

To end this section, two specific topics related to the legal context in Russia. The first topic is about quality control. The federal legislation and the government normative acts provide for procedures of quality control concerning both the form and content of reports and dissertations. The form of reports is defined by the National Standard GOST 7.32-2001 "The research report. Structure and rules of presentation", the form of dissertations by the National Standard GOST P 7.0.11-2011 "Dissertation and dissertation abstract. Structure and rules of presentation". As far as the content is concerned, reports and dissertations are peer-reviewed no less strictly than it is done for scientific articles or books. A dissertation would not be accepted for the conferment of the scientific degree if it is not accompanied by at least three written reviews by independent official opponents, that is, well-known scientists in the field. The head of the issuing organization would not sign a report if it is not discussed and recommended by the expert scientific and technical council, and unsigned reports are not accepted by CITIS.

The second topic concerns licensing. It is usual to consider two types of OA – gratis OA and 'libre' OA. 'Libre' OA means that the users are granted some additional rights as compared to just free online access called gratis OA. To be compliant with copyright law, 'libre' OA often specifies the additional rights in terms of Creative Commons licenses developed by the U.S. non-profit corporation Creative Commons for more than fifty jurisdictions all over the world.

The Russian Federation has not yet joined the Creative Commons community but Version 4.0 of the licenses released on November 25, 2013 acts as a single global license and needs no porting (adaptation) for national copyright jurisdictions. Now that a CITIS reading-room visitor may order a partial copy of a full-text GL document (report or dissertation) he/she is asked to sign a paper with a claim like: "For non commercial reuse" or "For research purposes only". But this paper has moral rather than legal power. In the future, if Russia accepts the Creative Commons regulations, this paper could be changed for, say, Creative Commons Non-Commercial license (CC-NC) allowing the licensees to copy, distribute, display, and perform the work and make derivative works based on it only for non commercial purposes.

Concluding remarks

Open access is essentially an international trend with a huge potential for information exchange. The idea of open access originated from the protest against the over-commercialization of STI. The old conflict between the author and public interests has turned into a conflict between some powerful international publishing houses and academic communities. In the search for alternatives two types of OA were suggested: the so-called "green" and "gold" roads. In the case of the green road, as applied to grey literature, a report or a dissertation is self-archived by the author or his/her institution using the personal or the institution site for free access. Here, the problem is permanent support for open repositories and their content preservation for the future. The gold road means that somebody (the author or his/her institution) pays article-processing charges to the publisher so that the latter allows free access to the publication. By definition, the gold road relates to commercial publishing and does not seem applicable to grey literature.

No doubt, technology plays a leading role in favor of OA. Internet, networking and personal computing technologies proved OA effectiveness and created a real OA explosion due to quick access to relevant sources, increased amount of readers, searches, hits, citations and therefore growing knowledge and impact. Today, the very term "OA" is inseparable from the Internet. However, as we showed above, OA to STI in general and to grey literature in particular did exist in the pre-Internet era and still exists in non-Internet forms like free access to STI collections in public libraries, reading-rooms of information centers and by means of interlibrary loan and document supply services.

While technology globally supports OA, legal and economic factors tend to set barriers to OA. Copyright law is the main obstacle in the way of OA to full-text reports and dissertations and copying of the texts in digital formats especially. Embargo periods for full-text and licensing (Creative Commons and others) may facilitate OA to deposited documents.

Also, a new business model of STI production and dissemination is crucial for the success of OA. Whatever "free OA" means, somebody must pay for the freedom of access. Contrary to commercial publishing where publishers' profit and activities are secured by subscribers, different models of OA suggest that the author, the author's institution, the state (tax-payers), sponsoring and funding organizations or whoever else must pay for the OA supporting expenses. These include not only the expenses to run the site and/or computer server but also funding the long-term archiving and preservation of the stored digital material for future generations. Who is to pay? That is the question and the answer strongly depends on each country's particular situation in science, education and STI. In modern Russia the state can and must be the main if not the only financial support of OA, at federal or local levels. An ethical argument is that as most of the scientific research in Russia is funded by the Federal State, that is, by taxpayers, the public has the right of free access to research results. As scientific authors can hardly secure a long-term preservation of their digital documents, the state-funded federal system with a centralized digital full-text collection appears as an optimal basis for successful OA development. The public support of STI and OA is realized as a part of Russian science funding. The main role of the state in science funding is to remain in Russia in the future.

Today, there is no doubt that OA has become the main vector of scientific communications in Russia. We conclude our paper with some suggestions to facilitate and accompany this development:

- The creation of a Russian language OA system similar to the Lund University journal directory DOAJ.
- The establishment of a nation-wide organization of an OA repository system, with registration, certification and functional

support of open repositories, similar to the German DINI network[10] or the European DRIVER infrastructure[11].

- The development of OA modules for integrated library systems with embedded DSpace, E-prints, E-Pub, Greenstone, etc., tools.
- The participation in international OA infrastructures and projects.

Having in mind the international readership of this chapter it must be said that most Russian publications, reports and dissertations are in the Russian language. This is why OA to these items supposes some knowledge of Russian. Since this has not been a widespread quality of foreigners, cross-national OA to Russian scientific production would need some more or less expensive translation tools. To overcome the language barrier in OA, international cooperation and special projects should be initiated. In particular we would suggest two actions:

- The promotion of Russian repositories amidst foreign academic communities.
- The promotion of and assistance in usage of foreign thematic and institutional archives through Russian language recommendations, manuals and instructions, statistics of usage, etc.

---

10 http://dini.de

11 http://www.driver-repository.eu

REFERENCES

Jeffery, KG 2006, 'Open access: an introduction', *ERCIM News* no. 64.

Parinov, S et al. 2013, 'A challenge of research outputs in GL Circuit: from OA to open use'. Paper presented at the *GL15 Fifteenth International Conference on Grey Literature*, CVTI SR, Bratislava, Slovak Republic.

Pavlov, LP 1998, 'The state and development of the Russian grey literature collection and dissemination centre', *Interlending & Document Supply*, vol. 26 no. 4, pp. 168-170.

Pavlov, LP 2002, 'La literatura gris de Rusia en el mundo de la información digital', *Ciencias de la Informacion*, vol. 33 no. 2, pp. 39-43.

Schöpfel, J & Farace, DJ 2010, 'Grey Literature', in *Encyclopedia of Library and Information Sciences, Third Edition*, eds MJ Bates & MN Maack, CRC Press, London, pp. 2029-2039.

Starovoitov, AV et al. 2012, 'Federal Information System on Grey Literature in Russia: a new stage of development in digital and network environment', *The Grey Journal*, vol. 8, no. 2, pp. 106-111.

Starovoitov, AV et al. 2014, 'Federal GL System input flow analysis', *The Grey Journal*, vol. 10, no. 1, pp. 33-37.

All websites accessed between March and April 2014.

Facts & Figures:
India

Country and Economy

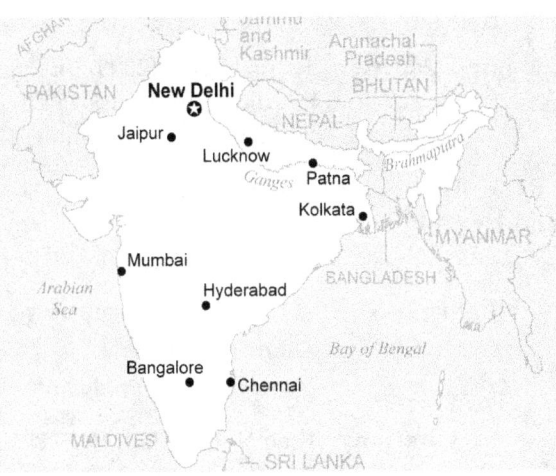

Capital	Name of Capital: New Delhi
Area	In km²: 3,287,267
Population Size	2013 Estimate: 1,252,139,596 Country Ranking: 2
Density	Per km²: 381
GDP (nominal)	In Billions of US$ (2014 estimate): 5,302,495 Country Ranking: 3
GDP per Capita	In US$ (2014 estimate): 4,209 Country Ranking: 117
Human Development Index	HDI (2012): 0.554 Country Ranking: 136

Research and Open Access

Scientists — Total Number (2009) (in thousand full-time equivalents): 154.8
Per Capita: 137 per 1 million

Expenditures on Research and Development — In Billions of US$ (2011): 36.1
% of GDP: 0.9%
Country Ranking: 9

Publications — Total Number (2013): 106,029
Country Ranking: 7
Number of Citable Documents: 98,968

Citations — Total Number (2013): 29,871
Country Ranking: 13
Citations per Document: 0.28
H-Index: 341

Journals — Total Number of Academic and Scholarly Journals (2014): 2,820
Journals with Impact Factor (2012): 122

Open Archives — Institutional Repositories: 59
Disciplinary Repositories: 7
Aggregating Repositories: 2
Governmental Repositories: 0

Open Access Journals — Total Number of Open Access Journals
- UlrichsWeb: 913
- DOAJ: 593

Overview

Open access in the world's largest democracy, India, is a success story. Several hundred peer-reviewed open access journals, institutional support by important research organisations, laboratories and universities, a growing number of open repositories, international programs, a favourable public climate and a prolific body of research studies on open access are evidence of this success.

The following chapter describes the development of open access, with many details on the policies and projects of the most important higher education and research institutions, such as the Council of Scientific and Industrial Research (CSIR), the Indian Council of Agricultural Research (ICAR) and governmental Department of Science and Technology (DST) and the Indian Institutes of Technology (IIT), and also NGOs and international institutions and private research laboratories.

Yet, only one percent of India's scholarly population of teachers, researchers and students appears to be concerned by open access so far. Researchers in general have positive attitudes towards open repositories, but even though they are aware of the benefits, they are reluctant to deposit their documents. Why is this so? The specific contribution of this chapter is the focus on studies on awareness and acceptance of institutional repositories and open access journals by Indian scientists.

The author, Sarika Sawant from the SHPT School of Library Science at the SNDT Women's University at Mumbai, also provides an overview of so-called predatory publishing, i.e. malpractices in open access journal publishing which has become a serious problem in India. Is this the price to pay for the success of open access journal publishing, as a kind of collateral damage? This cannot be; and the author shows some ways to deal with the problem.

Another interesting aspect in this paper is the link between open access projects, workload, job skills and professional training, with arguments for short-term courses to develop the abilities required for developing open access content creation and usage.

Sarika Sawant is affirmative – following her insights, the picture of open access in India looks very promising as policy makers are taking a keen interest in the development of the movement. Yet, she is more specific; for her, self-archiving in repositories (green road) appears to be reasonable and more promising than open access journal publishing (gold road) because the infrastructure is there and because it is less expensive, because it allows faster turnaround and is compatible with publishing in conventional journals. This is an interesting prognosis in line with open access experts like Stevan Harnad, and somehow in contradiction with the lobbying by commercial publishing and some national policies. But India is a land of contrast and diversity, where old cultural and religious traditions, great poverty and inequalities, industry, commerce, richness and high tech coexist. The future will show who is right, if open access just adds another contrast to India, if there is space for both green and gold, and which one will be the particular Indian contribution to the global movement.

About the Author

Sarika Sawant is Assistant Professor in SHPT School of Library Science at the SNDT Women's University in Mumbai, India. She has several years' experience teaching Library and Information Sciences at post graduate level. She holds a PhD in Library and Information Sciences on the institutional repository initiative in India. She is author of several papers and communications in international and national conferences and coordinated a research project on institutional repositories on women's studies in India and Canada. Sarika Sawant's research interests are in cataloguing, information processing, digital libraries, open archive initiatives, etc.

Open Access in India: Awareness and Acceptance of Institutional Repositories and Open Access Journals

Dr. Sarika Sawant

Introduction

In India today important amounts of scholarly research, including more than 600 peer-reviewed open-access journals, 46 institutional repositories, 5 repositories with electronic theses and dissertations (ETD) and 3 subject repositories are available to every researcher on his or her desktop, tablet or mobile. Open Access (OA) is a subject of discussion on online forums, on blogs, interviews, workshops, seminars, on public debates and meetings of higher authorities. It is also discussed in newspapers, general magazines, science and social science magazines to spread awareness about how OA is a threat to commercial publishers, about its impact on scholarly communication, its benefits, its developments, with lists of renowned OA publishers and even with warnings about predatory publishers. Even international organizations like UNESCO and the Commonwealth Educational Media Centre for Asia are interested in the OA movement in India and fund OA projects. Yet, only one percent of India's scholarly population of teachers, researchers and students appears to be concerned by OA so far.

The penetration of the Open Access concept in India

A decade ago in 2004 the Indian Institute of Science (IISc) launched India's first institutional repository. Simultaneously the first workshop on 'Open Access and Institutional Repositories' was organized under the aegis of the M. S. Swaminathan Research Foundation, Chennai, to train participants in uploading GNUEprints software on a Linux server. Two years later, a special session on Open Access (OA) was held at the 93rd Indian Science Congress in January 2006, which came up with the recommendation for the 'Optimal National Open Access Policy' (Sahu & Parmar 2006). The Ministry of Human Resource Development (MHRD) of India set up the 'Indian National Digital Library in Engineering Sciences and Technology (INDEST) Consortium' and encouraged members to set up e-print archives using appropriate OAI-compliant e-print software.

As the concept of OA percolated in India results were reflected in the form of the building of different types of repositories such as the Librarian's Digital Library (LDL) of the Documentation Research and Training Centre (DRTC), Bangalore; and OpenMed@ NIC, by the National Informatics Centre, New Delhi. India's first cross-institutional electronic thesis and dissertation repository (ETD) Vidyanidhi was developed by the University of Mysore. Later the NCSI-IISc created a Cross Archive Search Service for Indian Repositories (CASSIR), which harvests metadata via the OAI-PMH protocol from the registered OA repositories in India, and provides a web-based search and browse service with harvested metadata. CASSIR contains 63,000+ records from 24 Indian repositories.

From 2004 on, the number of OA users and developers communities increased, with LIS professionals, teachers and researchers. Some enthusiastic followers of OA started to organize workshops, seminars and conferences, and even OA Week celebrations became part of the ritual. OA is discussed by Yahoo groups, on mailing lists and blogs dedicated to the exchange of OA thoughts. As a result, the number of institutional repositories increased from 14 in 2007 to 45 in 2014 (Sawant 2013)[1].

---

1   See also http://cis-india.org/advocacy/openness/blog/open-access-to-scholarly-literature

Institutional repositories

The international directories of open repositories ROAR[2] and OpenDOAR[3] list 68 and 70 Indian institutional repositories (17 May 2014). However, some of them are no longer active and others are mere repetitions. After a careful comparison of both directories, it was found that there are 45 operational institutional repositories, together with three subject repositories and seven repositories with electronic theses and dissertations.

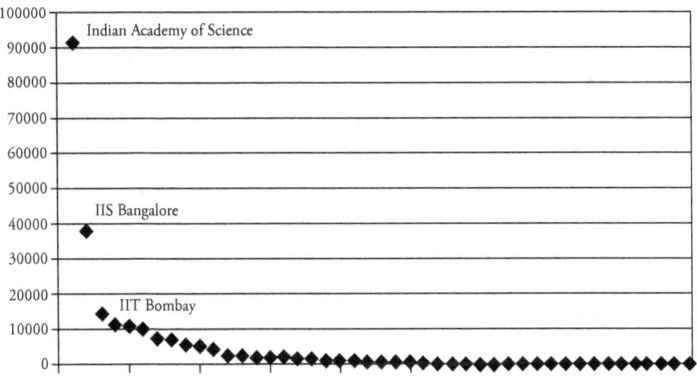

Figure 3.1: Ranking of 45 institutional repositories (N=number of items)

Institutional repositories generally contain journal articles, conference papers and reports, convocation reports and photos, annual reports, newspaper clippings and articles, newsletters, and other institutional publications. The most important higher education and research institutions have developed institutional repositories. The list includes seven CSIR[4] laboratories (R&D), four ICAR[5] laboratories, four universities, four agriculture laboratories, three Indian Institutes of Technology (IIT), two governmental Department of Science and Technology laboratories (DST), a society, an NGO, a college, an

---

2   http://roar.eprints.org
3   http://opendoar.org
4   Council of Scientific and Industrial Research http://www.csir.res.in/
5   Indian Council of Agricultural Research http://www.icar.org.in/

international institution and a private research laboratory. In addition to these, there is one cross-institutional repository ePrints@MoES launched by the Ministry of Earth Sciences (MoES) that contains 345 documents from the MoES research community, i.e. the Ministry, its affiliate institutes and programs (Jaykanth et al. 2012).

The very first repository was launched in 2004 by the Indian Institute of Science, Bangalore, and now contains about 38,000 documents. The most important repository is hosted by the Indian Academy of Sciences, Bangalore, with more than 90,000 documents. It is unique in the world because it contains papers by all its fellows, both living and deceased. The Academy was also the first in India to adopt OA for its journals. For instance, its physics journal, Pramana, became OA as far back as 1998[6]. Together, the 45 institutional repositories contain 231,835 items, with a median size of 835 items which means that half of them have less than 1,000 deposits (Figure 3.1). Table 3.1 presents the ten most important repositories.

Host institution	Items
Indian Academy of Sciences	91,953
Indian Institute of Science	37,296
IIT Bombay	14,099
Indian Institute of Management , Ahmedabad	11,122
Indian Institute of Astrophysics	10,621
Central Marine Fisheries Research Institute	9,670
International Crops Research Institute for the Semi-Arid Tropics -	7,362
Central Food Technological Research Institute	6,834
National Aerospace Laboratories	5,687
Raman Research Institute	5,025

Table 3.1: The ten most important institutional repositories (17 May 2014)

---

6   http://euroscientist.com/2013/09/open-access-an-opportunity-for-scientists-around-the-globe/

The seven ETD repositories contain together more than 25,000 theses (table 3.2). The most important is Shodhganga with nearly 16,000 items, while the other sites are rather small (median size = 2,046 ETD). Three of them are cross-institutional, with ETD from different universities (Shodhganga, IIS and Explorations) while the others are all related to specific institutions, such as ethesis@nitr, the OA theses repository of the National Institute of Technology Rourkela.

Name/Host institution	Items
Shodhganga@INFLIBNET Centre	15,737
ethesis@nitr	3,090
Theses and Dissertations of Indian Institute of Science	2,240
Mahatma Gandhi University	1,852
University of Agricultural Sciences, Dharwad	1,414
Explorations – OA Repository of Indian Theses (CSIR)	937
Vidyanidhi, University of Mysore	n/a
Total	25,270

Table 3.2: Repositories with electronic theses and dissertations

Three subject repositories have been launched in India but without much success. Openmed@NIC contains 2,904 documents in biomedical sciences, the Librarians Digital Library provides access to 490 items in library and information sciences, while for OpenAgri, a repository in agriculture, no updated figures are available.

All these repositories are OAI-compliant which allows for metadata harvesting and aggregating by central services (Jaykanth & Minj 2012) such as for example Search Digital Libraries (SDL), SJPI (Scientific Journal Publishing in India) Cross Journal Search Service, Search Engine for Engineering Digital-repositories (SEED), Open J-Gate and Knowledge Harvester@INSA.

The National Institute of Technology Rourkela was the first institution to decide an OA mandatory policy, with an obligation for scientists to deposit their publications in the institutional repository. In 2014, ten institutions are listed in the international Registry of

OA Repositories with Mandatory Archiving Policies ROARMAP[7]. Recently, the Indian Council of Agricultural Research (ICAR) announced a mandatory OA policy for its 97 research laboratories and for all funded research projects; its implementation is in progress[8].

Research studies on Indian institutional repositories

Several studies by Indian scientists and scholars describe the situation and development of institutional repositories, in particular in terms of their number and size, type of software, content and item typology, policies etc. (Ashok Kumar 2009; Babu et al. 2012; Krishnamurthy & Kemparaju 2011; Lihitkar & Lihitkar 2009; Mukherjee & Mal 2012; Sawant 2011a; Sawant 2011b).

Other articles discuss the experience of developing and maintaining institutional repositories (Doctor 2007; Jayakanth et al. 2012; Jayakanth et al. 2008; Jobish et al. 2005; Krishnamurthy 2005; Kumar 2012; Laxminarsaiah & Rajgoli 2007; Madalli 2003; Patel et al. 2006; Sutradhar 2006).

But there are only a small number of studies that focus on researchers' awareness, attitudes, usage, content contribution and problems associated with institutional repositories or any other types of repositories. Below are some important studies with significant contributions on these topics.

Sawant (2012) investigated knowledge, practice and opinions about institutional repositories (IR) among the users of institutions with IR. This included scientists, faculty members, students, etc., who may or may not be using the IR facility. It was found out that there was a lack of awareness of IR among the institutional members, so it needs urgent attention to promote the repositories. Also, among those who are aware of IR through links provided on institutions' websites some had deposited only a few documents to their IR. The most important reason for deposits was found to be the preservation of documents for the future. Users were willing to help the library and computer service staff of the institution in managing the IR.

Sahu & Arya (2013) analyzed the awareness of OA publishing among researchers and faculty members of Indian institutions and

---

[7] http://roarmap.eprints.org/

[8] http://icar.org.in/en/node/6609

evaluated the development of OA initiatives in India. It was found that the awareness about such OA information resources and initiatives among the research community is increasing.

Das (2013) conducted a research study to determine the level of understanding of OA, participation in OA knowledge creation and training needs of researchers of Jawaharlal Nehru University (JNU) in India. The study revealed that respondents showed limited use of OA literature as well as limited contribution in OA content creation.

Gutam et al. (2013) conducted a study to find out attitudes and awareness about OA among the researches of the National Agricultural Research System (NARS). The results showed that nearly 50% were not aware of what OA is. However, 62% of them were interested in deposits of post-prints in repositories but not pre-prints and datasets. 32% strongly agreed that with OA, the quality would improve and 42% agreed that it would be easier to get hold of papers. This suggested that with increased OA, advocacy and repositories establishment would solve the accessibility issues in NARS.

Manjunatha & Thandavamoorthy (2011) explored researchers' attitudes towards deposit in OA IR as a mode of scholarly publishing. The study revealed that the majority of the science, technology and medicine scholars were aware of and in favor of deposit in IR. However, the humanities and social science researchers (except for those from the arts) were found to have a low level of awareness of the IR but were interested in contributing with their research work and had a positive attitude towards providing free access to scholarly research results of their university. Literature related to arts and humanities in Indian repositories is insignificant as compared to science and technology.

Beena & Archana (2011) documented and shared the real time experience of managing and sharing of intellectual wealth of academia of Cochin University of Science & Technology by using open source platforms. They also explored different intellectual information resources in the current era and suggested cost effective strategies for implementing new OA tools and technology for effective managing of intellectual informatics.

Kenneway (2011) conducted a survey amongst a group of authors who were already favorably inclined towards OA, through their experience as customers of InTech, an OA Publisher. When they were asked how important OA was to them, 9.8% answered that it was unimportant or not important at all, which was relatively high compared to responses from other countries. On the other hand, only 68.7 % said that OA was very important and important for them, which was below the average response level from the other countries.

Sawant (2010) estimated the number and the rate of growth of digital documents of Indian institutional repositories for the year 2007-2008. It was observed that during the year 2007, the average rate of growth per IR per month was 3.10%. In 2008, the average rate of growth per IR per month was 5.70%.

All these studies have shown that researchers generally have positive attitudes towards contribution to repositories, but even though they are aware of its benefits, they are reluctant to deposit documents in the repositories. Unless and until it is made compulsory for them to deposit in repositories, repositories will not be filled up. The University Grants Commission (UGC[9]) in India has made obligatory the deposit of soft copies of PhD theses to the respective university that gets uploaded by the library in Shodhganga immediately. Similarly there should be mandates to deposit research reports of UGC/ICSSR/DST/CSIR funded projects before further proposals can get approval. The best solution is to decide on a national mandate of deposition of publicly funded research reports in subject and or institutional repositories or on personal websites.

Looking at these studies, there are certain areas of research that need more attention by Indian researchers such as OA mandates, authors' intellectual property rights, licensing issues, etc.

Open Access journals: India a leader at global front

There are two ways to achieve OA: one is called the "green road" by archiving pre-prints and post-prints in repositories and the other is the "gold road" by publishing research findings in OA journals. The best option for researchers is the "gold road". India provides opportunity to researchers from all around the world to opt for the "gold road" by publishing their research findings in almost 600 OA journals produced by Indian publishers. India's share in OA journal publishing is 6%. The international Directory of OA Journals (DOAJ)[10] shows 590 journals but there might be more journals which may not have been registered

---

9   http://www.ugc.ac.in/

10 http://doaj.org/

in DOAJ (Sawant 2009). But as those journals do not follow Open Archives Initiative Protocol for Metadata Harvesting (OAI-PMH), it will be difficult for them to get discovered by search engines.

India has a significant and growing contribution in the field of OA journals that is reflected in table 3.3. According to DOAJ India is at 4th position while it ranked at the 9th position in 2005 (Lewis 2012).

RANK	COUNTRY	NUMBER OF JOURNALS	IN %
1	United States	1,203	12.22
2	Brazil	907	9.22
3	UK	609	6.19
4	India	590	6.00
5	Spain	516	5.24
6	Egypt	440	4.47
7	Germany	333	3.38
8	Romania	297	3.02
9	Italy	287	2.92
10	Canada	262	2.66

Table 3.3: India's contribution to DOAJ (2014; % for first 10 countries)

Out of these 590 OA journals, 254 are completely free of charge for readers and authors (no article processing charges (APC), 43%), 255 do charge for article processing (43%) and 78 apply conditional charges that may depend on research funding, review procedures etc. (figure 3.2).

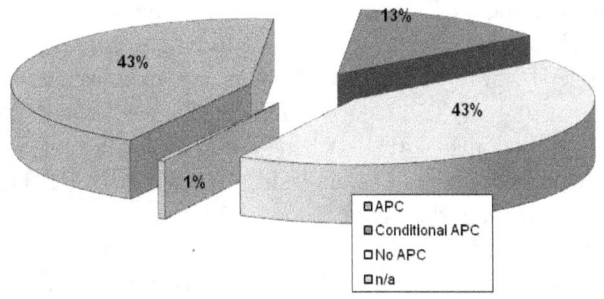

Figure 3.2: Article processing charges per OA journals in % (N=590).

Some Indian OA journals are published by public services and institutions such as the Indian MEDLARS Centre of the National Informatics Centre with 65 journals in the field of biomedical information, the NISCAIR online periodicals repository (18 journals), the Indian Academy of Sciences (11 journals) and the Indian National Science Academy (4 journals). Other journals are published by commercial, corporate publishing houses as Medknow Publications (335 journals), Indianjournals.com (26 journals) or Kamla-Raj Enterprises (7 journals). One part of these private companies has been criticized as "predatory publishers"; we will come back to this aspect below.

STUDIES RELATED TO ATTITUDES OF INDIAN AUTHORS TOWARDS OPEN ACCESS JOURNALS

Several research papers explore the current status of OA journals in India, mainly focusing on the number of journals, OA typology (full or hybrid OA, author payment model), host organization, indexing, etc. (Bandi et al. 2013; Das 2009; Goudar et al. 2013; Pandita 2005; Sahu 2006; Sawant 2009; Jandoo & Vedamurthy 2012). Few people evaluated OA journals in different disciplines, such as library and information sciences, biomedical sciences or mass media (Rufai et al. 2011; Husain & Nazim 2013). Some papers were published on actual usage and users of OA journals and publishing in OA journals.

Bhat (2009) conducted a study to provide an overview of OA publishing by five important research institutes in India, for the period from 2003 to 2007 and based on Scopus records. The study showed that these five institutions produced 17,516 research articles in 4,232 journals, with a small but significant percentage in OA journals. The Indian Institute of Science (IIS) published 8.26% of its research output in OA journals, All India Institute of Medical Sciences (AIIMS) 19.37%, Baba Atomic Research Centre 4.84%, Indian Institute of Technology (IIT) Delhi 3.04% and Indian Institute of Technology (IIT) Kharagpur 3.26%. The majority of these OA journals are published in India. The medical institutions are contributing more of their publications to OA journals, compared to other institutions.

Marimuthu (2013) conducted a survey with 1,220 scientists and engineers from 16 different aerospace organizations of Bangalore. The objective was to analyze usage patterns of OA journals in this specific research field. The results revealed a preference for journals on technology and engineering and for the ICAST, NAL Gateway of Free Journals, but also significant differences between the selected organizations ($P < 0.05$). Obviously, in this specific domain of aerospace, usage patterns and preferences of OA journals are not approximately the same.

Lone et al. (2013) studied the contribution of authors of Indian institutions to the OA movement in the field of medicine. They identified journals in medical sciences indexed in Elsevier's Scopus database to spot India's share in the OA movement. The study covered data from the five year period 2005–2009, from various Indian institutions including universities, medical colleges, hospitals, clinics and other medical structures. The findings showed that between 2005 and 2009 Indian authors produced 10,410 papers in medical sciences in OA journals. The study further revealed that AIIMS was the main contributing institution to the OA movement in India.

Butdisuwan & Reddy (2012) surveyed authors of Mahasarkham University (MSU), Thailand and University of Hyderabad (UoH), India, to evaluate their understanding of OA and their involvement in OA publishing. The results showed that less authors published their papers in OA journals than in non-OA journals. The main reasons were the missing peer-review and low journal impact factor. Other reasons were high costs of publishing (article processing charges) and missing support (encouragement) from their institution.

Madhan & Arunachalam (2011) surveyed the contribution of Indian authors in high impact international OA journals, i.e. all seven Public Library of Science (PLoS) journals, 10 BioMed Central (BMC) journals and Acta Crystallographica Section E: Structure Reports. It was found that Indian crystallographers have published more than 2,000 structure reports in Acta Crystallographica, second only after China in number of papers but with much better citations per paper average than USA, United Kingdom, Germany, France, China and South Korea. India's contribution to BMC and PLoS journals, on the other hand, was less important.

All these studies show that the Indian researchers' awareness of and contribution to OA journals is increasing, not only in science and technology but also in other disciplines. In the case of medical science literature, Manikandan & Wani (2010) have recommended that the funding bodies such as the Indian Council of Medical Research

(ICMR), and the governmental Department of Biotechnology (DBT) and Department of Science and Technology (DST) should join PubMed Central (PMC) to form PMC India so that every scientist who has received grants could (and should) deposit the full text of their papers in order to make them freely accessible to everyone.

The dark side of Open Access journal publishing

Many new OA publishers are springing up in India and China, where increasing numbers of researchers are creating large publishing markets. Pressure to publish is often intense in developing countries, and vanity presses could attract unscrupulous researchers keen to pad out their CVs.

Beall (2012) coined the term 'predatory publishers', which means publishing counterfeit journals to exploit the OA model in which the author pays[11]. These predatory publishers are dishonest and lack transparency. They aim at duping researchers, especially those inexperienced in scholarly communication. They set up websites that closely resemble those of legitimate online publishers, and publish journals of questionable and rather low quality. Many purport to be headquartered in the United States, United Kingdom, Canada or Australia but really hail from Pakistan, India or Nigeria.

Perhaps nowhere else are these abuses more acute than in India, where new predatory publishers or journals appear each week. They appear because of the market need — hundreds of thousands of scientists in India and its neighboring countries need to get published to earn tenure and promotion (Bohannon 2013). To find out malpractices in OA publishing, Bohannon (2013) submitted a spoof paper with major scientific flaws, easily identifiable by any researcher with adequate experience, to 304 OA journals from different publishers such as Elsevier, Wolters Kluwer, and Sage, identified from the international Directory of OA Journals (DOAJ) and Beall's journals list. Of these, 157 journals had accepted and 98 rejected the manuscript. Thirty-six of them had commented, recognizing those flaws, finally 16 accepted the paper after commenting. Of the 157 journals which accepted the article, 64 are based in India. This sting

---

11 http://scholarlyoa.com/

operation has brought to light the poor editorial quality and peer-reviewing process of these OA journals.

Malpractices in journal publishing are a serious problem in India. Beall's weekly updated list contains many Indian publishers, and according to Madhan[12] more than 130 such journals sprouted in India during 2012-2013. India, unfortunately, is also home to predatory conferences as well. As the Indian University Grants Commission (UGC) made it compulsory for every scholar or researcher to earn points by publishing articles not only in journals that are indexed, with peer-review and/or impact factor but also in journals categorized without peer-review, indexed or not, the pressure for publishing in such kinds of journals has become even worse. Doing this, UGC is increasing the quantity but not the quality of research. This new format may or may not be sustainable in the future but at present it is pushing every scholar belonging to a university to publish articles in any which way. Predatory publishers are aware of this situation and take full advantage by publishing so called author paid OA journals. To limit the problem, UGC has recently published guidelines that say that only those research articles shall be accepted which are published in journals approved by specific subject committees of the university. Such subject-wise lists of journals, periodicals and publishers must be made available on the universities' website[13].

Another way to reduce such malpractices is to inform researchers, scholars and students about so called predatory publishers, for instance in the framework of initial and continuous education programs for scientists and librarians, or by writing short columns on innovations in and threats to the scholarly communication and OA movement in institutional newsletters.

The OA Scholarly Publishers Association (OASPA[14]) promotes a uniform definition of OA publishing, best practices for maintaining and disseminating OA scholarly communications, and ethical standards. OA publishers who are members of OASPA are expected to adhere to the Professional Code of Conduct which specifies that company contact information, editorial board, fees and charges,

---

12   See http://tonyhey.net/2014/06/03/a-global-view-of-open-access-part-6/

13   http://www.ugc.ac.in/pdfnews/8539300_English.pdf

14   http://oaspa.org/

licensing policies, instructions to authors, process and policies related to peer-review shall be clearly outlined on the journal or publisher web site. Authors must check the details before submission of an article to journals. Actually, more than 100 organizations and individuals are members of OASPA, but none of them from India. The problem of predatory publishers can get worse in the near future but can be solved if OA becomes completely free for authors as well as for its users. This is an ideal OA, termed as Diamond or Platinum OA, and will give a new direction to OA publication (see Sau 2013).

Current updates on Open Access movement in India (May 2014)

Actually 1,084 Indian authors have published OA books or chapters with InTech[15] which is a pioneer and the world's largest multidisciplinary OA publisher of books covering the fields of science, technology and medicine, with 86,447 authors from 3,079 institutions from 149 countries.

The international E-LIS repository[16] currently contains 804 documents from Indian professionals and researchers in library and information sciences.

During the national conference on 'Opening up by closing the circles: strengthening the OA in India' (October 13, 2013) at Jawaharlal Nehru University (JNU) to mark the OA Week celebration, the central library of JNU presented the package of 5,000 digitized ETDs by JNU scientists to the director of INFLIBNET for uploading in Shodhganga[17] (Jawaharlal Nehru University 2013).

Speaking at the national conference ROUTE 2013, 'Reaching out to users through technology', R.R. Hirwani, head of the CSIR Unit for Research and Development of Information Products, said that their laboratory will set up a central harvester, which will harvest the metadata of other CSIR repositories (30 out of 38 have already launched an IR), and will make it openly accessible. He later added that CSIR will take a lead along with other scientific agencies to form a National OA Policy, including legislation, if necessary to mandate

---

15   http://www.intechopen.com/

16   http://eprints.rclis.org/

17   http://shodhganga.inflibnet.ac.in/

the availability of output of publicly-funded research in the public domain (Indian Express 2013).

At the International Conference on Digital Libraries (ICDL 2013) Dr. Arora, director of INFLIBNET, announced the development of a central repository 'Shodhsagar' under NME-ICT through which all the IRs can be harvested into INFLIBNET's proposed central repository (Tata Energy Research Institute 2013).

The Electronic Publishing Trust offers awards for individuals in developing and transition countries who have made significant advances to the cause of OA and the free exchange of research findings. For the year 2013, the joint award winner was Muthu Madhan, Manager of the library and information services at ICRISAT, Hyderabad.

Madalli has proposed in 2013 three general Principles of OA about free knowledge, scholarship and its acceptance. Following Madalli, a systematic and persistent approach to OA will pave the way to true 'Democratization of Knowledge'[18].

During the OA Week in October 2013, ICRISAT developed an OA booth which is a portal for its researchers.

The Indian initiative Knimbus is a dedicated knowledge discovery and collaborative space for researchers and scholars[19]. Knimbus helps researchers find and access 13,000 commercial and OA journals, 1.8 million e-books, 27,000 online courses, millions of theses, conference proceedings, magazine and news articles and much more. It enables single window discovery of all e-resources subscribed by individuals and institutions, combined with collaboration, personalization and social features to experience higher research productivity and gain valuable insights.

Impact factors of Indian OA journals are rising: There is a considerable increase in the number of Indian journals having IF ≥ 1.0. Out of 47 Indian OA journals in JCR-2011, 13 had an IF greater than 1.000 in 2011 (Gunasekaran & Arunachalam 2012).

The OA repository "Publications of Fellows of the Indian Academy of Sciences" is ranked at position 262 by Webometrics[20] (world

---

18   http://drtc.isibang.ac.in/xmlui/bitstream/handle/1849/512/General_Principles_OA.pdf?sequence=1

19   http://www.knimbus.com/open

20   http://repositories.webometrics.info/en/Asia/India

repositories ranking), with 91,953 total number of documents, while the IISC Bangalore is at position 345 with 38,000 documents.

Indian publishers and their copyright policies in case of self-archiving: 47 Indian publishers are registered in the SHERPA/ROMEO[21] database of publishers, with altogether 684 journals. 610 journals are green category journals which allow self-archiving of pre-print and post-print or publisher's version/PDF, 52 blue category journals which allow archiving of post-print (i.e. final draft post-refereeing) or publisher's version/PDF, and 22 white category journals where archiving is not formally supported.

The new Directory of OA Books (DOAB[22]) increases discoverability of OA books by inviting academic publishers to provide metadata of their OA books to DOAB in order to maximize dissemination, visibility and impact. Two years after its launch unfortunately, none of the Indian publishers have joined DOAB.

Open J-Gate[23] of Informatics, India provides a database of journal literature, indexed from 3,000+ OA journals, with links to full text at the publisher sites. Currently it provides links to over 5,320,569 open-access articles.

With support from the Ministry of Human Resource Development (MHRD), the National Council of Educational Research & Training (NCERT) launched on 13 August 2013 the National Repository of Open Educational Resources (NROER) portal, a free online repository of NCERT courseware. MHRD has also funded the National Program on Technology Enhanced Learning (NPTEL) that provides E-learning through curriculum based online web and video open educational resources (OERs) in engineering, science and humanities streams. NPTEL has developed 700 video courses and these can be accessed through the NPTEL website, YouTube, and two Indian channels, Ekalavya and Gyan Darshan. It is also available on DVDs and hard disks.

---

21 http://www.sherpa.ac.uk/

22 http://www.doabooks.org/

23 http://openj-gate.org/

Capacity building & Open Access curriculum for researchers and library and information professionals: Indian initiatives

The last decade has seen a couple of studies on the perception, attitudes and awareness of students, scientists and librarians towards OA publishing and archiving. At the same time, several seminars, conferences, workshops and training courses were conducted in all parts of India to raise awareness and to teach professionals how to develop institutional repositories with OA software, metadata harvesting, etc. However, all these initiatives remain rather informal, without certification.

In a rapidly changing OA landscape, Swan (2012) and Urs (2011) identified gaps of knowledge and suggested short courses to develop the skills required for the creation and usage of OA content. Based on a survey of OA training opportunities, Urs (2011) proposed a model syllabus for OA. More recently, Mishra (2013) conducted a two-phase Delphi study in order to develop a draft curriculum for a graduate level course in OA. The study identified as core content for library and information professionals at graduate level the following topics: introduction to OA, history and its impact, copyright and licensing, OA policy development, models for funding, major OA initiatives, OA journal publishing, repository software and OA information retrieval. Yet, this content can also be an object of LIS Master level dissertations, or it can be taught outside of the formal training program, for instance as part of continuing education[24].

Perspectives

After twenty years of the OA movement, India's share in institutional repositories worldwide is 2.5% (60 out of 2,355[25]) and 6% for OA journals[26]. More repositories and journals will be launched in the near future. For scientists, access to scientific information is crucial for writing research papers or project proposals or to stay up to date

---

24 http://cemca.org.in/ckfinder/userfiles/files/Chan_Capacity%20Building_Open%20Access%20Final1.pdf

25 ROAR, May 2014

26 DOAJ, May 2014

with recent advances in their field (Jain 2013). Lewis (2012) estimated that gold OA could account for 50% of all scholarly journal articles sometime between 2017 and 2021, and 90 percent of articles by 2020 or 2025. If this comes true, then there is absolutely no more need to ask for full text access or order copies as today. In fact today, Indian researchers often try to request copies of published papers directly from the authors because of lacking library resources (Gaulé 2009). OA could change this situation.

Quality and impact of OA journals are increasing. Björk (2012) found that OA journals indexed in the Web of Science and/or Scopus are approaching the same scientific impact and quality as traditional subscription-based journals, particularly in life and medical sciences and for author-paid journals with article processing charges.

Higher authorities in India, like CSIR and ICAR are seriously considering OA mandates for their affiliated institutions and programs. Mandatory policies for OA archiving is important to enhance scholars' awareness of and participation in OA by depositing documents to the repositories and adjusting themselves to this innovative scholarly communication chain. But Xia (2012) found that mandatory policy may have little or no visible impact on the growth of repositories. Obviously, one size does not fit all and the same approach may not work for all open repositories. In order for OA mandates to perform well, the institutional policy must reflect the needs of the faculty. A national OA mandate can be helpful insofar as it creates a global framework for local and institutional initiatives and guides the adaptation of repositories' mandates to specific institutional needs and interests.

The increasing number of institutional repositories concerns essentially life sciences, science, technology, engineering, agriculture science and medicine while social sciences, arts and humanities are underrepresented. Consequently, a significant part of India's academic community in arts and humanities takes less advantage of the OA movement. The solution could be institutional or subject repositories where authors of this discipline self-archive their papers. If the National Assessment and Accreditation Council (NAAC), an autonomous body established by the University Grants Commission (UGC) of India which assesses and accredits institutions of higher education such as colleges and universities, would support institutional repositories and self archiving as an evaluation criteria, then many more scientists and institutions would be involved.

The National Knowledge Commission recommended in 2007 that research articles published by Indian authors receiving any government or public funding must be made available under OA and should be archived in the standard OA format on his/her website[27]. But hardly anyone has implemented this recommendation so far. The UGC decided on a mandatory policy for electronic theses and dissertations in order to increase their visibility, availability and impact (Minimum Standards & Procedure for award of M.Phil. / Ph.D Degree, Regulation, 2009). All university libraries affiliated to the UGC must deposit their theses and dissertations on the Shodhganga ETD repository. Online access to electronic theses through digital repositories will not only ensure easy access and preservation of Indian doctoral theses but will also improve the standard and quality of research, especially by reducing duplication of research since there is no national catalogue of PhD theses. This could be a model for national mandates of other leading research institutions and organizations in India.

To extend OA further, the self archiving route appears to be reasonable particularly in developing countries. Setting up institutional archives does not cost much today. The software is free and the technological infrastructure, such as the server and the internet connectivity, is already available in most institutions. About a decade ago, the scarcity of computers and high bandwidth access in many developing countries would put them at a disadvantage. But now prices have gone down. Thus, OA archiving is even more promising than OA journals. It is less expensive, allows faster turnaround, and is compatible with publishing in conventional journals (Arunachalam 2013). However, in larger institutions such as universities OA may still remain a problem. For instance, even though the creation and maintenance of repositories is mainly done by the library staff, sometimes this additional workload is not considered and evaluated as a part of their job, so that it becomes difficult to cope with routine library work. This may be true with other smaller institutions, too. It is also evident from the ROAR directory that many repositories are launched but not maintained. It would be advisable at least to create one post in universities completely dedicated to the creation and

---

27   http://www.knowledgecommission.gov.in/downloads/documents/wg_open_course.pdf

maintenance of institutional repositories, to guarantee their sustainable development. Also, the education of competent professionals in OA training courses could contribute to this development.

Urs (2011) suggested that we need a new strategic approach to OA. Given the landscape and the prospects, perhaps it is time to move beyond the first generation of the OA movement and scope the potential and possibilities of OA for the next decade. The second phase of the OA movement might be capacity building by developing courses, through strategic training of professionals able to take the OA movement to the next level.

Acknowledgement

I would like to thank all my Indian OA scholar friends who provided me with information required for the present study.

References

Ashok Kumar, N 2009, 'Institutional repositories in India'. Paper presented at the *National Seminar on Strategic Information Management in the Digital Era*, Tamil Nadu, India.

Babu, PB et al. 2012, 'Rationale of institutional repository categories and IR development challenges in India', *Library Review* vol. 61, no. 6, pp. 394–417.

Bandi, S et al. 2013, 'Open access scholarly publishing in India: a scientometric perspective of DOAJ'. Available from: http://eprints.rclis.org/21191/

Beall, J 2012, 'Predatory publishers are corrupting open access', *Nature*, vol. 489, no. 7415, pp. 179–179.

Beena, C & Archana, NS 2011, 'Open access movement for managing intellectual informatics', *Library Herald*, no. 49, pp. 221-228.

Bhat, M 2009, 'Open access publishing in Indian premier research institutions', *Information Research*, vol. 14, no. 3.

Björk, BC & Solomon, D 2012, 'Open access versus subscription journals: a comparison of scientific impact', *BMC Medicine*, vol. 10, no. 1, p. 73.

Bohannon, J 2013, 'Who's afraid of peer review?' *Science*, vol. 342 no. 6154, pp. 60–65.

Butdisuwan, S & Reddy, ER 2012, 'Open access and scholarly communication: authors perspectives in Thailand and India with special reference to MSU and UoH', *Journal of Indian Library Association*, vol. 48, no. 3, pp. 31-43.

Das, AK 2009, 'Open access to research literature in India: contemporary scenario', *International Society for Scientometrics and Informetrics*, vol. 5, no. 1, pp. 9-14.

Das, AK 2013, *Open access awareness and practices of JNU researchers: report of a baseline survey*. Available from: http://cemca.org.in/ckfinder/userfiles/files/Anup_CEMCA_Report_Final_combined.pdf

Doctor, G 2007, 'Knowledge sharing: developing the digital repository of SIPS', *VINE*, vol. 37, no. 1, pp. 64–73.

Gaulé, P 2009, 'Access to scientific literature in India', *Journal of the American Society for Information Science and Technology*, vol. 60, no. 12, pp. 2548–2553.

Gibbs, PE 2013, 'The dark side of open access', *Prespacetime Journal*, no. 4, pp. 91–93.

Goudar, IRN et al. 2013, 'Best practices for the development of institutional repository: a case study of ePrints@UoM'. Paper presented at the *National Seminar on Emerging Trends in ERMS in College Libraries*, Mysore, India.

Gunasekaran, S & Arunachalum, S 2012, 'Correspondence', *Current Science*, vol. 103, no. 7.

Gutam, S et al. 2013, 'Awareness and attitude towards open access in India's National Agricultural Research System'. Available from http://works.bepress.com/sridhar_gutam/18

Husain, S & Nazim, M 2013, 'Analysis of open access scholarly journals in media & communication', *DESIDOC Journal of Library & Information Technology*, vol. 33, no. 5, pp. 405-411.

Indian Express 2013, 'CSIR to create open access repositories'. *Indian Express* 13 March.

Jain, NC 2013, 'Open access ensures effective information retrieval of medical literature in e-databases', *Indian Journal of Community Medicine*, vol. 38, no. 1, pp. 1–3.

Jandoo, T & Vedamurthy, A 2012, 'Open access to scientific information: a review of initiatives', *DESIDOC Journal of Library & Information Technology*, vol. 32, no. 3, pp. 255-260.

Jawaharlal Nehru University 2013, 'Conference report', in *National conference on opening up by closing the circles: strengthening the open access in India*. New Delhi, India.

Jayakanth, F & Minj, F 2012, 'Federated search service for OAI-compliant open-access repositories in India', in *International*

Conference on Trends in Knowledge and Information Dynamics (ICTK–2012), Bengaluru, Karnataka, India.

Jayakanth, F et al. 2008, 'ePrints@IISc: India's first and fastest growing institutional repository', *OCLC Systems & Services*, vol. 24, no. 1, pp. 59–70.

Jayakanth, F et al. 2012, 'Setting up an open access digital repository: a case study', *Annals of Library and Information Studies*, vol. 59, no. 1, pp. 16-24.

Jobish, P et al. 2005, 'Etd@IISc: a DSpace-based ETD-MS and OAI compliant theses repository service of Indian Institute of Science'. Paper presented at *ETD 2005: Evolution Through Discovery*, Sydney, Australia.

Kannan, S & Gowri, S 2014, 'A study with spoof paper–reflection of reviewing processes in open–access journals', *Journal of Pharmacology & Pharmacotherapeutics*, vol. 5, no. 1, p. 70.

Kenneway, M 2011, 'Author attitudes towards open access publishing'. Available from: http://www.intechopen.com/public_files/Intech_OA_April1.pdf

Krishnamurthy, M 2005, 'Digital library of mathematics using DSpace: a practical experience', *SRELS Journal of Information Management*, vol. 42, no. 3, pp. 245-256.

Krishnamurthy, M & Kemparaju, TD 2011, 'Institutional repositories in Indian universities and research institutes: a study', *Program: Electronic Library and Information Systems*, vol. 45, no. 2, pp. 185–198.

Kumar, S 2012, 'Establishment of institutional mechanism for building national repository in health sciences', *DESIDOC Journal of Library & Information Technology*, vol. 32, no. 3, pp. 277-284.

Laxminarsaiah, A & Rajgoli, IU 2007, 'Building institutional repository: an overview', *OCLC Systems & Services*, vol. 23, no. 3, pp. 278–286.

Lewis, DW 2012, 'The inevitability of open access', *College & Research Libraries*, vol. 73, no. 5, pp. 493-506.

Lihitkar, S & Lihitkar, R 2009, 'A study of major institutional repositories in India'. Available from: http://eprints.rclis.org/14234/

Lone, MI et al. 2013, 'Leading medical institutions of India: a study of open access publication in the field of medicine', *International Journal of Science, Engineering and Technology Research (IJSETR)*, vol. 2, no. 6.

Madalli, D 2003, 'A digital library of library and information science using Dspace'. Paper presented at the *DRTC Workshop on Semantic Web*, Bangalore, India.

Madhan, M & Arunachalam, S 2011, 'Use made of open access journals by Indian researchers to publish their findings', *Current Science*, vol. 100, no. 9, pp. 1297-1306.

Manikandan, S & Vani, I 2010, 'Restricting access to publications from funded research: ethical issues and solutions', *Journal of Postgraduate Medicine*, vol. 56, no. 2, p. 154.

Manjunatha, K & Thandavamoorthy, K 2011, 'A study on researchers' attitude towards depositing in institutional repositories of universities in Karnataka (India)', *International Journal of Library and Information Science*, vol. 3, no. 6, pp. 107-115.

Marimuthu, G 2013, 'Open access journals and its use patterns among the aerospace scientists and engineers of Bangalore', *International Journal of Advances in Engineering & Technology*, vol. 6, no. 3, pp. 1109-1122

Mishra, S 2013, 'Towards open access curriculum for researchers and library and information professionals'. Available from: http://cemca.org.in/ckfinder/userfiles/files/Anup_CEMCA_Report_Final_combined.pdf

Mukharjee, B and Mal, B 2012, 'India's efforts in open access publishing library', *Philosophy and Practice*. Avaiable from: http://www.webpages.uidaho.edu/~mbolin/mukherjee-mal.htm

Pandita, N 2005, 'Open access journals in India'. Paper presented at the *International Seminar on Open Access for Developing Countries*, Salvador, Bahia, Brazil.

Patel, Y et al. 2006, 'Institutional digital repositories/e-archives: INFLIBNET's initiative in India', in *Conference Proceedings*, ed. MG Sreekumar, EssEss Publications, New Delhi, pp. 312–318.

Rufai, R et al. 2012, 'Open access journals in library and information science: the story so far', *Trends in Information Management*, vol. 7, no. 2.

Sahu, DK & Parmar, R 2006, 'The position around the world: open access in India', in *Open Access: Key Strategic, Technical and Economic Aspects*, ed. N Jacobs, Chandos Publishing, Oxford, pp. 26-32.

Sahu, DK 2006, 'Open access publishing in the developing world: economics and impact. Asia Commons'. Paper presented at the *Asian Conference on the Digital Commons*, Bangkok, Thailand.

Sahu, DK & Arya, SK 2013, 'Open access practices in India', *Library Hi Tech News*, vol. 30, no. 4, pp. 6–12.

Sau, K 2013, 'Facts about journal publishing in open access policy', *The Indian Journal of Medical Research*, vol. 138, no. 6, pp. 1029–1030.

Sawant, S 2009, 'The current scenario of open access journal initiatives in India', *Collection Building*, vol. 28, no. 4, pp. 159–163.

Sawant, S 2010, 'Growth of Indian institutional repositories', *ISST-Journal of Advances in Librarianship*, vol. 1, no. 1, pp. 69-75.

Sawant, S 2011a, 'Institutional repositories in India: a preliminary study', *Library Hi Tech News*, vol. 28, no. 10, pp. 6–10.

Sawant, S 2011b, 'IR system and features: study of Indian scenario', *Library Hi Tech*, vol. 29, no. 1, pp. 161–172.

Sawant, S 2012, 'Indian institutional repositories: a study of user's perspective', *Program: Electronic Library and Information Systems*, vol. 46, no. 1, pp. 92–122.

Sawant, S 2013, 'Past and present scenario of open access movement in India', *The Journal of Academic Librarianship*, vol. 39, no. 1, pp. 108–109.

Sutradhar, B 2006, 'Design and development of an institutional repository at the Indian Institute of Technology Kharagpur', *Program: Electronic Library and Information Systems*, vol. 40, no. 3, pp. 244–255.

Swan, A 2012, *Policy guidelines for the development and promotion of open access*, UNESCO, Paris.

Tata Energy Research Institute 2013, 'Conference bulletin', in *ICDL(2013)-Vision 2020: Looking Back 10 Years and Forging New Frontiers*.

Urs, S 2011, 'Directory of open access education and training opportunities'. Available from: http://www.unesco.org/new/fileadmin/MULTIMEDIA/HQ/CI/pdf/UNESCO-OA-ET-Report-WithAppendix-final-Urs.pdf

Xia, J et al. 2012, 'A review of open access self-archiving mandate policies', *Portal: Libraries and the Academy*, vol. 12, no. 1, pp. 85–102.

All websites accessed between April and June 2014.

Facts & Figures:
China

Country and Economy

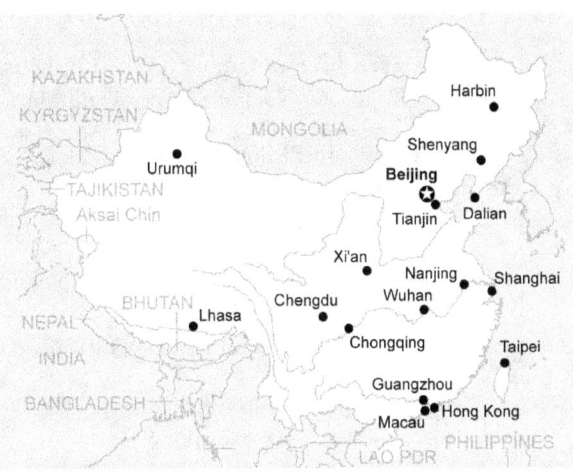

Capital	Name of Capital: Beijing
Area	In km²: 9,596,931
Population Size	2013 Estimate: 1,385,566,537 Country Ranking: 1
Density	Per km²: 144
GDP (nominal)	In Billions of US$ (2014 estimate): 14,578,977 Country Ranking: 2
GDP per Capita	In US$ (2014 estimate): 1066 Country Ranking: 169
Human Development Index	HDI (2012): 0.699 Country Ranking: 101

Research and Open Access[1]

Scientists	Total Number (2009) (in thousand): 1,152.3 Per Capita: 863 per 1 million
Expenditures on Research and Development	In Billions of US$ (2012): 296.8 % of GDP: 1.97 Country Ranking: 2
Publications	Total Number (2013): 425,677 Country Ranking: 2 Number of Citable Documents: 416,292
Citations	Total Number (2013): 127,012 Country Ranking: 2 Citations per Document: 0.3 H-Index: 436
Journals	Total Number of Academic and Scholarly Journals (2014): 4,454 Journals with Impact Factor (2012): 96
Open Archives	Institutional Repositories: 39 Disciplinary Repositories: 0 Aggregating Repositories: 0 Governmental Repositories: 0
Open Access Journals	Total Number of Open Access Journals • UlrichsWeb: 75 • DOAJ: 51

---

1   Figures without Hong-Kong and Taiwan

Overview

China, often considered as the "Middle Empire" and the centre of the universe, is different from other countries. Not only does it look back on more than 5,000 years of civilisation with several key innovations like paper, gunpowder, the compass and banknotes, but also through its philosophy of Confucianism and Taoism it has exerted a determining influence on the culture and art of governance in East Asia and well beyond. Today, China with the highest population worldwide and a rapidly growing economy is no longer the "sleeping giant"; it has become a global player at all levels, be it in finance, business, diplomacy, military or environment.

China is different from other countries, and so is the following paper. Instead of a general overview, it provides original results of a recent survey of open access journals published in China. Why focus on journals? OA journals in China started late, but they developed rapidly. The international directory DOAJ contains only a few Chinese journals, a tip of the iceberg, while the hidden part, i.e. the real number is much higher. In fact, less than 5% of the OA journals are indexed by DOAJ whereas the rest remain virtually invisible and unknown to the international research community.

This is where the interest of the following chapter lies. The author, Dehua Hu from the Central South University in Changsha, conducted the first systematic and comprehensive survey of Chinese OA journals in 2013. The results provide a unique picture of the actual situation in the OA publishing market, with detailed information not only on their number, disciplines, periodicity and age but also on their business and dissemination models, their regional origins, online services and back-files. Moreover, the study reveals some significant tendencies over the last five years. Today, OA journals represent 20% of all Chinese journals in sciences, technology and medicine (only 10% in 2009), most of which are hosted and distributed in PDF on independent websites. In a certain way, the Chinese OA journal publishing landscape made up of many different local projects and initiatives may be compared to hundreds of blooming flowers, compared to other countries with great national platforms such as Brazil with SciELO or France with OpenEdition. Why is this so? Where will they go?

This is the last part of the paper. Based on the empirical results and on his experience with the international OA movement, Dehua

Hu suggests some elements for a proactive public policy on OA. For instance, he suggests modifying the system of accreditation and control of new scientific journals, developing networking and partnerships, fostering the quality control of papers and improving the protection of the authors' intellectual property. Yet, in quite a Chinese way, he also insists on the equilibrium between public, publishers' and authors' interests, and he insists on the need for co-existence between print and digital journals and different dissemination models. No revolution, but a new state of stability and development. Yet, his conviction is obvious: for the development of Chinese science and the visibility of its research output, open access is not only interesting but necessary.

The reader may find other interesting topics and information on regional distribution and the link between economy and OA publishing, on the responsibility for older content, on the importance of private (corporate) initiative (quite different from the Russian approach, for instance) or on language barriers, a crucial problem for many emerging and developing countries but often underestimated (if not simply forgotten) by the mainstream publishing industry and the OA movement. Other questions remain open, such as the need for interoperability and standards.

Today, China is already the second producer of scientific articles after the USA and far ahead of other countries. For the Chinese, scientific journal publishing is critical. Their problem is impact, in terms of visibility, usage and citations. Will OA journal publishing contribute to this impact? The future will tell. But one thing is certain – any development in China will have an influence well beyond the country's frontiers.

By the way, do you know Changsha? Have you ever heard of this town? Nearly 2,000 years old, Changsha is the capital and largest city of the Hunan province, with more than seven million people living there, more than all the inhabitants of Los Angeles, San Diego, San Francisco and Sacramento put together. They have the tallest building in the world, called Sky City One. The South Central University ranks amongst the best 100 universities worldwide in the field of engineering sciences. If you have never heard of Changsha, it does not matter, but think about it – this is just a part of the visibility issue mentioned above and the reason why the chapter is of special importance in this book.

About the Author

Dehua Hu is professor of Library and Information Sciences in the Department of Medical Information of the Central South University in Changsha, China. He holds an M.A. in Library and Information Sciences and a Ph.D. in Social Medicine and Health Management. From 1996 to 1998, he was Library Assistant at the Hunan Medical University Library. Since 1998, he has been lecturing at the Central South University in Changsha. From 2004 to 2006, he contributed to the construction of a public health emergency response command system for the Chinese Ministry of Health. From 2011 to 2012, he was visiting scholar at the Johns Hopkins University, Baltimore, Maryland. He is the author of several papers on medical information, academic publishing, scientific journals and open access.

OPEN ACCESS IN CHINA: THE DEVELOPMENT OF OPEN ACCESS JOURNALS

Dehua Hu

INTRODUCTION

In December 2001, a meeting on "accelerating progress in the international effort to make research articles in all academic fields freely available on the Internet" was held in Budapest, marking the start of the Budapest Open Access Initiative (BOAJ)[2]. Two years later, the Berlin Declaration consolidated the idea that scientific publications should be open to users. Since then, an increasing number of organizations and individuals support the open access (OA) initiative, and more and more resources are being made freely available on the Internet. In 2014, nearly 10,000 journals from more than 130 countries were published in open access, and their number has more than doubled in the last four years[3].

OA journals in China started late, but they developed rapidly. The international directory DOAJ contains 75 Chinese journals with 24 journals published in Taiwan, while the total number was only 37

---

2   http://www.soros.org/openaccess

3   Directory of Open Access Journals http://www.doaj.org

in 2010. However, the number published is much higher. The OA platform Chinese Science Paper Online includes 271 journals in natural science, 189 in engineering and technology, 89 in medicine and health, 55 in agricultural science and 185 in social sciences and humanities; and their number is increasing year by year.

The China Association for Science and Technology (CAST) has been evaluating Chinese journals for many years, including their OA status (see the last update CAST 2012). However, a systematic survey of OA journals has been missing so far. Therefore, we conducted a comprehensive survey of Chinese OA academic journals in 2013. The following chapter will present the main results – number, characteristics and problems of OA journals in 2013, trends since 2009 – and propose appropriate strategies for the further development of OA journal publishing in China.

Literature review

Chinese scholars first began to study OA journals in 2004, analyzing a wide range of topics ranging from OA journal development and academic quality to the organization, preservation, copyright issues and usage of OA journals. In recent years, more and more of these studies have focused on Chinese OA journals.

From 2006 on, with financial support from the China Association for Science and Technology (CAST), W.H. Cheng and co-workers conducted a series of surveys and evaluated the development of the science and technology OA journals sponsored by CAST[4]. At the same time, this research group analyzed the open access (OA) publishing status of Chinese scientific journals, based on the 1,608 journals covered by the Chinese S&T Journal Citation Report (2005 edition) (Cheng & Ren 2007, 2008). From this database, they identified 91 journals offering full OA and a further 139 offering delayed OA. Data collected at three different time points (January 2006, July 2006, and January 2007) showed that the OA status of these journals was not stable; some OA journals subsequently became non-OA. Most of the Chinese OA journals are not part of a larger aggregation but published independently. A plurality of OA journals are published in the fields of medicine and biology. Between 2008 and

---

4 See the CAST reports 2008-2012.

2010, Cheng and his colleagues further reported on the development of OA journals sponsored by CAST (Cheng et al. 2008, 2009, 2010). Zhang & Pan (2010) addressed the quantity, distribution, and properties of the full text of the Chinese OA scientific and technology journals indexed by *A Guide to the Core Journals of China* (2008 edition) and the Chinese S&T Journal Citation Report (2009 edition). They identified the main OA-related challenges faced by Chinese science and technology journals, and they explored the factors that have influenced the development of OA. Their report offers some effective strategies and suggestions for OA Chinese science and technology journals with regard to improving their influence and building a favorable macro-environment for OA.

Another study focused on OA journals in computer science and technology in China (Zhang 2010). For the 25 computer science journals included in the China S&T Journal Citation Report (2009 edition), this study analyzed the numbers of journals with OA and evaluated their online forms, text format, the need for back-tracking to open the full text, and the lag time occurring before papers became available. Among the 25 full-text journals, 10 (= 40%) offered OA; three journals were available through OA back to the first year of publication. The study also found that the peak time for full retrospective OA was reached after 2002; eight of the journals' online editions and printed versions were synchronous and opened immediately.

An earlier study tried to map the landscape of OA publishing of university journals in China (Shen et al. 2008). Using data from the Chinese S&T Journal Citation Report (2007 edition), they identified 34 OA journals fulfilling three criteria: they were free (OA), refereed, and scholarly.

Exploring the viability of this novel type of OA publishing in universities, Geng & Huang (2010) assessed the status of the 158 Chinese OA journals available in 2010. They pointed to the following shortcomings of university-affiliated Chinese OA journals: decentralization, duplication of content, an inadequate level of openness and depth, discontinued availability of issues, and an uneven distribution of disciplines.

Chen et al. (2011) conducted a first scientometric analysis of the dynamics, domains and the current situation of OA journals in the

Chinese Social Science Citation Index, exploring academic distribution and applying visualization techniques (scientific knowledge mapping).

The impact of Chinese OA journals was evaluated by Jin et al. (2012). They selected 797 journals out of 1,086 OA journals ranked by the Chinese S&T Journal Citation Report (2010 edition) and analyzed the journals' academic and network influence by two indicators, e.g. impact factor and immediacy index.

Reviewing the controversy about OA and governmental policies, Cui (2013) suggest that OA journals may become mainstream in the future but that OA and traditional journals might as well co-exist so that academic information would be retrieved in many different ways.

How and why do researchers accept OA journals? Based on a questionnaire survey and regression statistics, Qu & Shi (2014) showed that condition, experience, familiarity with OA journals and professional status had a significant effect on the acceptance of OA journals, while discipline, effort expectancy and article processing charges (APC, publication fees paid by the author) had no significant effect.

All these studies contributed to a better understanding of OA journals in China. However, they are limited in range or are confined to some particular scholarly domain. To our knowledge, no systematic and comprehensive research that has examined all of the OA journals published in China has been conducted up to now. Filling this gap is the objective of our paper.

Methodology

Our survey sample contains scholarly journals that were indexed by the China National Knowledge Infrastructure full-text databases (CNKI) in 2009 and 2013, covering natural science and engineering and technology (including basic science, engineering, agricultural science, medicine and health, information technology) and humanities and social science (including philosophy & humanities, social science, economics and management science).

We applied four criteria for the selection of the survey sample:

1. Relevance of the content. The journal must be included in the CNKI database, indexed strictly according to the Chinese Library Classification and compliant with standard characteristics of academic, scholarly journals (editorial policy, submission requirements, abstracts, etc.).

2. Free access to website. The journal must own a suitable URL, and readers should automatically have all the authority necessary to allow them to visit the website via the Internet. The home page should be easily accessible under normal operating conditions; if not, we should consider network jams. No registration should be needed, or the free access should appear after registration.
3. Free open access. Considering the current circumstances in China, we reduced the level of this requirement to less than full OA, limiting our requirement to the availability of access to download or read the full text for free.
4. Regular publication. The journal should be published regularly and employ a continuous series number. The frequency of publication should be at least one issue per year.

The survey was designed to identify the journal's website using the Google search engine and to collect information directly on the OA journal's website about different variables, such as the scientific fields, the periodicity, language, etc.

Results and discussion

Number of OA journals

At the end of 2013, the CNKI database contained 8,601 academic journals. 1,370 journals could be identified as OA journals, representing nearly 16% of all journals (Table 4.1).

	Total number of CNKI journals		Number of OA journals		In %	
	2009	2013	2009	2013	2009	2013
Natural Science and Engineering	5,154	5,250	538	996	10.44	18.97
Humanities and Social Sciences	2,960	3,351	146	374	4.93	11.16
Total	8,114	8,601	684	1,370	8.43	15.93

Table 4.1: Number of OA journals in China (October 2009 and December 2013)

Whereas the total number of academic journals has increased by 6% since 2009, the number of OA journals has doubled during the last four years (+100%). In the field of natural science and engineering, the portion that were OA journals in 2013 was nearly 19%, while their portion in the humanities and social sciences category was about 11%. All of the OA journals had corresponding print versions.

These results indicate that the number of OA journals increased at a relatively rapid rate in all domains in China. Yet, Table 4.1 also shows that natural science and engineering journals tend to be more open to OA publishing than those in the humanities and social sciences. This difference may reflect the nature of the journals, since those in the humanities and social sciences are more likely to adhere to the traditional publishing model.

Scientific disciplines

All academic journals of the CNKI database are indexed according to the Chinese Library Classification with their main scientific discipline. Our survey reveals that OA journals cover the whole range of the 22 scientific disciplines of the Chinese Library Classification, except for "Marxism, Leninism, Mao Tse-tung Thought". Figure 4.1 shows the ten main disciplines covered by OA journals.

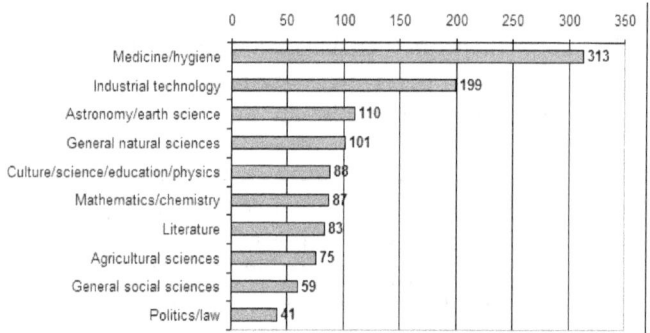

Figure 4.1: Scientific disciplines of Chinese OA journals in 2013 (top ten, total number=1,370)

The most important discipline is medical sciences and public health with 313 OA journals, i.e. 23% of the total number of OA journals, followed by industrial technology (engineering), astronomy/earth science and natural sciences. The top ten disciplines of Figure 1 represent together 84% of all OA journals while the other 16% include economics, philosophy, transportation, arts and other disciplines.

Between 2009 and 2013, the number of OA journals increased in almost all disciplines. However, the speed of growth was different. Figure 4.2 shows some of the top ten disciplines.

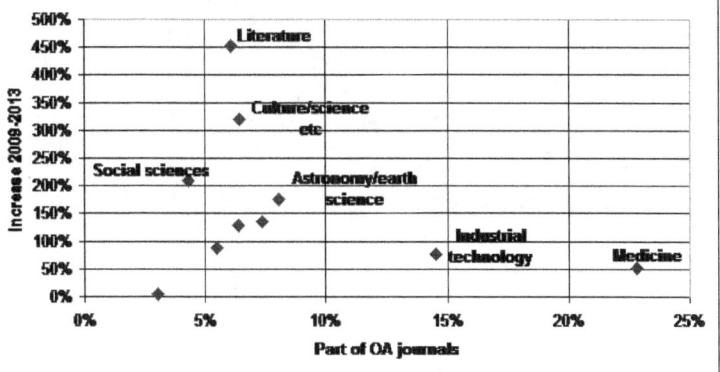

Figure 4.2: Number and growth of Chinese OA journals 2009-2013 (top ten disciplines, total number=1,370)

The average increase between 2009 and 2013 for all OA journals was +100%. The most important growth rates have been registered by literature (+453%), culture/science (+319%), general social sciences (+211%) and astronomy/earth sciences (+175%), whereas the number of OA journals in the more important disciplines like medicine and industrial technology increased at a slower pace (+52% and +78%).

Regional distribution

China is made up of 31 provinces, autonomous regions and municipalities. In 2013, OA journals were mostly published in Beijing (34%) and Shanghai (7%). Nevertheless, all other provinces, regions and municipalities (in particular Jiangsu, Hubei, Guangdong, Shanxi, and Sichuan) have their own OA journals. Furthermore, the survey results reveal two tendencies: on the one hand, the concentration of OA journals in Beijing and Shanghai is slightly decreasing, a tendency in favor of the other regions. On the other hand, the growth rate appears to be related to the global economic situation, with a high increase in the developed South China while development in the Western regions is rather slow.

Age of OA journals

There are very few "native" OA journals in China, and nearly all OA journals were created and launched as print journals years before the digital OA version. Figure 4.3 presents the year of creation for all OA journals identified in 2009 and 2013, from 1913 to 2013.

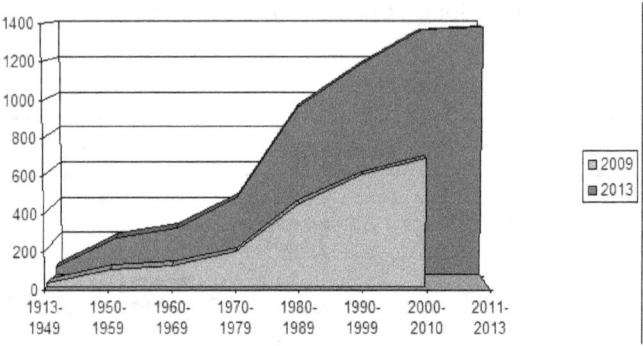

Figure 4.3: Year of creation of Chinese OA journals (2009 and 2013)

Figure 3 shows that from the beginning, the development of Chinese OA journals has its origins in traditional print journal publishing and reflects the history of Chinese scientific journals. Before 1950, China founded very few scientific journals, and the number of journals that have been preserved and survived until now is even less. From 1950 to 1960, China made great efforts to apply socialist principles to journal publishing, and the government's "Hundred Flowers" campaign promoted large numbers of scientific and technical journals. In the next decade, as a result of ten years of chaos and the Cultural Revolution, the development of China's scientific and technical journals slowed down. But then, especially between 1980 and 1990, political and economic reforms in China and the opening up of the country led to an extensive development of scientific journals, and this growth continues today.

So it is not surprising that two-thirds of Chinese OA journals were launched between 1980 and 2010 while the percentage of recently created titles is insignificant (1%). Figure 3 also shows the effort to transform older print journals into digital OA journals between 2009 and 2013. In particular, the number of journals created before 1980 and transformed into OA products increased between 2009 and 2013 from 147 to 429, and their portion grew from 27% to 31%.

Periodicity

Most of the OA journals are published 6 (bimonthly) or 12 (monthly) times per year. Together, these titles with medium periodicity represented 78% (2009) and 82% (2013) of all OA journals (see Table 4.2).

PERIODICITY		NB (2009)	IN % (2009)	NB (2013)	IN % (2013)
High	Weekly	3	0.44	7	0.51
	3/month	6	0.88	23	1.68
	2/month	40	5.85	64	4.67
Medium	Monthly	249	36.40	511	37.30
	Bimonthly	283	41.37	608	44.38
Low	4/year	101	14.77	151	11.02
	2/year	2	0.29	3	0.22
	Annual	0	0	3	0.22
Total		684	100	1,370	100

Table 4.2: Periodicity of OA journals (2009 and 2013)

The portion of journals with low periodicity is slightly decreasing, especially for those titles with four issues per year (15% in 2009, 11% in 2013) while the portion of journals with higher periodicity, i.e. two or more issues per month, remains more or less stable. In 2013, three OA journals were published in annual volumes (*Confucianism Collection Forum*, *Public Management Research*, *Shanghai Astronomical Observatory of Chinese Academy of Sciences*).

Language distribution

Most of the OA journals are published in Chinese (96%), and their number is increasing rapidly.

LANGUAGE	2009		2013	
	NUMBER	IN %	NUMBER	IN %
Chinese	637	93.13	1,313	95.84
English	47	6.87	53	3.87
Bilingual	0	0	4	0.29
Total	684	100	1,370	100

Table 4.3: The language distribution of OA journals (2009 and 2013)

While the number of OA journals published in English increased very slightly and at a low level, from 47 to 53, four bilingual journals with articles in Chinese and English have been launched since 2009, including *Guizhou Literature & History Series, Sculpture, Space Medicine & Medical Engineering*, and *Control Theory and Applications*. However, DOAJ only indexes 51 Chinese OA journals, of which 33 are published in English and eight journals are bilingual. Obviously, Chinese OA journals published in Chinese are not represented in DOAJ, because of the language barrier. Support from international OA journal platforms would be needed to increase their visibility and improve their academic impact.

Dissemination models

Based on the nature of their first-level online domain and their dissemination system, Chinese OA journals can be divided into five categories: (1) single independent online journals where each journal has its own independent domain and website, (2) associated online journals where two or more journals share the same Internet domain and server instead of running their own website, (3) funding-supported online journals where the journals' content is available on the main website of a funding institution, (4) subject information network-supported online journals where the content is available on a main website supported by a subject information-related company (scientific association or network, learned society, etc.), and (5) journals disseminated on a foreign publisher's network platform.

OA SYSTEM	2009		2013	
	NUMBER	IN %	NUMBER	IN %
(1) Independent	277	40.50	978	71.39
(2) Associated	57	8.33	112	8.17
(3) Funding institution	177	25.88	102	7.45
(4) Network	168	24.56	169	12.33
(5) Foreign publisher	5	0.73	9	0.66
Total	**684**	**100**	**1,370**	**100**

Table 4.4: Models of OA systems (2009 and 2013)

As Table 4.4 shows, most Chinese OA journals (71%) are independent and provide their content on their own website, via an individual Internet domain. Also, their number and importance increased rapidly, at the expense of institutional and network platforms, which saw their portion decline from 50% in 2009 to 20% in 2013.

The portion of associated OA journals with two or more journals sharing the same Internet domain remained stable at 8%. Finally, so far the dissemination of Chinese OA journals on foreign publishers' platforms is insignificant, below 1%. Obviously, Chinese journal publishing bodies and communities prefer autonomous and independent solutions for the transition to OA. But only a small part of them are indexed in international databases and directories, such as DOAJ or Indian J-Gate (Chen & Chen 2013).

Internet domains and supporting institutions

More than half of all Chinese OA journals are disseminated on servers with the two Internet top-level domains .com (30%) and .net (24%).

Domain	2009		2013	
	Number	In %	Number	In %
.ac	53	7.75	94	6.86
.edu	95	13.89	232	16.93
.com	210	30.70	406	29.64
.gov	24	3.51	47	3.43
.net	179	26.17	326	23.80
.org	50	7.31	103	7.52
.cn	64	9.36	144	10.51
other	9	1.32	18	1.31
Total	**684**	**100**	**1,370**	**100**

Table 4.5: Online domains of Chinese OA journals (2009 and 2013)

Table 4.5 shows that a large number of OA journals have chosen .com as their top-level domain name, resulting in 210 (31%) in 2009 and

406 (30%) in 2013. Most of them are sponsored by research institutes, associations or learned societies, but their digital publishing services are provided by commercial information companies, such as *Journal of Plant Ecology* founded by the Chinese Plant Society and the Plant Research Institute of the Chinese Academy of Sciences.

Next, 179 (26% in 2009) and 326 (24% in 2013) journals have the first-level online domain name .net. These journals are mainly sponsored by institutes and organizations similar to .com OA journals, such as the *Chinese Optics Journal Network* or the *Principle Medicine in China*.

The OA journals with first-level domain names of .edu were mostly supported by colleges and universities. For instance, the *Journal of Zhenjiang High Commissioner* was launched by the Zhenjiang College. Between 2009 and 2013, the portion of these OA journals increased slightly from 14% to 17%.

The other top-level domain names are less important. The OA journals with .org (7%) are mostly sponsored by associations and societies, while journals with .ac (7%) are published by research institutes, like *Geological Sciences* published by the Research Institute of Geology and Geophysics of the Chinese Academy of Sciences. 3% (.gov) are sponsored by government authorities, such as the *Chinese Zhejiang Province Party School Paper* created by the Chinese Zhejiang Province Party Committee and the Zhejiang Administration School.

Our results show that the main first-level online domain names of Chinese OA journals are .com and .net, and they indicate that the focus of Chinese OA journals development has shifted from the establishment of OA journals to the provision of information-oriented services.

This new focus is beneficial to OA journal publication and distribution. Research institutes, associations and societies are able to make use of information companies' technology to address their own technical deficiencies, a trend that has been observed in Chinese OA journals in recent years. This development appears to be steady and stable.

Search functions

In 2009, of all the 684 OA journals, 371 journals provided search functions, accounting for 54% of the total. Of these, 174 journals offered a simple search box, sometimes with more search options, such as keywords, author, title, abstract and content. The other 197 supported more advanced search functions, such as limits for dates, volumes, issues and pages.

The portion of journals with simple or advanced search functions increased in 2013 to 951 journals (69%), such as the *Journal of Aeronautical Materials, Literature Area (Original Version), Chongqing Architecture* and others. In conclusion, the proportion of OA journals offering search functions increased in 2013, an increasing percent of OA journals provide more comprehensive services and are more concerned about the users' needs. However, 31% of the journals in 2013 do not support any search functions, and readers can only browse the articles through volumes or items provided on the website, a matter of considerable inconvenience to readers.

Online submission systems

266 (39%) of the 684 OA journals offered an online submission system in 2009. In these journals, authors could log on to the online submission page by registering and then conduct related operations and view the current status of their manuscripts. The portion of these journals increased slowly to 573 (42%) in 2013.

The other journals did not support online submission; they were usually supported by subject information websites or belonged to *Sciencepaper Online, Chinese Optics Journal Network* or the *Principle Medicine in China* platform. Comparing the data of 2009 and 2013, we can see that even if the portion of OA journals supporting online submission had increased, the online submission systems of Chinese OA journals websites still need to be improved.

Full-text accessibility of back files

We presented above the age of OA journals, including the fact that most of the Chinese OA journals had been created initially as print journals, mainly between 1980 and 2010. So what can be said about the online free availability of the journals' back files, i.e. the digitized print archives and former native digital articles?

Figure 4 shows the full-text availability of the 1,370 OA journals in 2013. Availability is cumulative. In 2013, all journals (100%) provided access to the papers published in 2013 (current year) and nearly all (98%) also provided access to papers published one year before, in 2012.

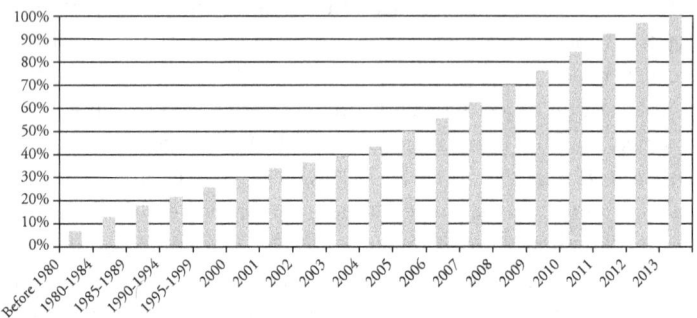

Figure 4.4: Availability of OA full-text (in 2013, N=1,370 journals)

Figure 4.4 shows the availability of older articles in full-text. In 2013, 77% of the journals made available up to five years of their content, 44% up to ten years, and 26% up to fifteen years. 97 journals (7%) offer volumes and issues in digital formats and OA that had been published in print before 1980. Different variables impact this availability, such as the year of going digital, digitization projects of print archives (back files) and the age of the journal.

The effort to augment openly available content can be measured when the 2013 data are compared to the survey results four years ago. In 2009, the percentage was much lower: only 64% of the journals made available up to five years of their content, 24% up to ten years, and only 18% up to fifteen years.

In 2009, *Acta Physica Sinica* was the earliest OA journal to make archival content freely available, 76 years back, followed by the *Journal of Mathematics* (73 years). In 2013, the earliest journals with available full-text are *Acta Meteorologica Sinica* (83 years back) and *Acta Physica Sinica* (80 years). There are many more Chinese OA journals with a long span of full-text availability in natural sciences than in social sciences and humanities. In addition, 108 (16%) of the 684 journals in 2009 had all their back files online, from the first issue of the first volume to the most recent issue, and this part increased since then to 327 (24%) of the 1,370 journals in the 2013 sample.

Timing online full-text delivery

Are the print and digital versions of the journals published at the same time or not? Only a very small number of journals (1-2%) provide pre-print versions ahead of the print edition. An increasing number–251 journals (39%) in 2009 and 649 (47%) in 2013 – published both versions at the same time. Yet still, about half of all OA journals disseminate the digital version subsequent to the print edition, with a delay of one (22%), two (8%) or three issues (21%) in 2013. But these delays have been diminishing since 2009, and the part of OA journals publishing their online version with a maximum delay of one issue increased between 2009 and 2013 from 63% to 71%.

Format of online full-text

In which format do Chinese OA journals deliver their articles? The overwhelming number of journals (76%) do this in the reader- and print-friendly PDF format (Table 4.6). This percentage is even higher if we add those journals that offer PDF along with HTML (11%). In 2009, more than one-third of the journals (37%) disseminated their content exclusively in HTML as web pages, but their number decreased and represented only 12% in 2013. The number of OA journals with other formats is insignificant.

Format	2009		2013	
	Number	In %	Number	In %
PDF	407	59.50	1,049	76.57
HTML	250	36.55	166	12.12
PDF&HTML	11	1.61	152	11.09
Other	16	2.34	3	0.22
Total	**684**	**100**	**1,370**	**100**

Table 4.6: Format of online full-text

PDF files are based on PostScript Language Image Model which ensures accurate print quality by faithfully reproducing each character, color and image of the original manuscripts and at the same time, occupying smaller space than the original files. The pages can be quickly displayed simultaneously with great convenience when downloading the files on the Web. Therefore, it is widely used by OA journals.

In addition, statistics show that compared with 2009, OA journals in HTML and other formats had the tendency to transfer into PDF format, which resulted in OA journals with PDF and HTML format getting a greater proportion for adapting to users' needs. This reflected the format evolution of OA journals which took the actual demand as a reference.

Summary

A quick growth on a low level

The number of China's scientific OA journals is increasing rapidly but their part of the total number of Chinese scientific journals remains rather low. Although the number of Chinese OA journals reached 1,370 in 2013 and is still growing fast, the OA journals represent only 16% of all Chinese scientific and technical journals, with a ratio higher in natural sciences and engineering technology (19%) than in social sciences and humanities (11%).

So far, many print journals have not taken into account the actual need for OA and continue with their traditional operating systems, management models and so on. Also, there is a deficit of projects and internal driving forces necessary to develop new business models and metrics for performance evaluation, to deal with new readership and intellectual property issues, and to lead the transition from print to OA. New strategies are needed for further development.

Regional and disciplinary inequalities persist

The survey data reveals that the development of Chinese OA journals is quite imbalanced in terms of regions and disciplines. Chinese OA journals are mainly concentrated in eastern regions and a small part of the central region, primarily Beijing, Shanghai, Jiangsu, Hubei, Guangdong, Shanxi and Sichuan, while the majority of the central regions and the provinces, autonomous regions and municipalities of the western regions have very few OA journals. The development of OA journals is closely related to the economic, scientific and technical level of each region, and these differences remain stable over the observed time period.

Regarding disciplines, most OA journals cover medicine and public health, industrial technology, astronomy and earth sciences and general natural sciences. These scientific fields are relatively popular, being the focus of academic attention, public funding and economic interest. In some ways, the development of OA reflects the importance of a discipline, and again, this situation did not change significantly between 2009 and 2013.

Only few native OA journals

Many Chinese OA journals were launched between 1980 and 1999, at the high period of academic journal publishing in China, and only very few are real native OA journals with no print past. Most of the OA journals are derived from print journals. The lack of new, native OA journals is probably related to a mandatory national "approval system" where most countries of the world have only national registration systems, without formal approval before the launch. This "approval system" makes the creation of native OA journals more difficult, impeding the prosperity and development of China's OA journals, and the limitation of the "approval system" has not improved since 2009.

The language barrier

Most OA journals were published in Chinese and only a small portion of them were in English. The percentage of bilingual OA journals with Chinese and English content is steadily growing but stilll too small to be significant. As international directories and search tools such as the DOAJ focus on English content, China's OA journal publishing remains to some extent behind a language barrier. Therefore, China should increase the number of OA journals published in English and fully take into account the importance of Chinese-English dual-language publishing, in partnership with international academic publishers and network platforms providers, in order to improve their visibility and develop their international impact for the exchange and dissemination of academic results.

Improved periodicity

At present, China's OA journals are mainly published bimonthly, monthly or quarterly. During the last several years, the publishing periodicity improved to some extent, with ten-days and weekly journals slightly increasing and quarterly and biannual journals declining. However, the periodicity still needs to speed up to facilitate instant publication.

Better web functionalities

The portion of OA journals without web-based search functions is diminishing but, at 30%, it is still too high. Some journals continue to rely on websites offering information about the subject and providing only e-magazine format, which is inconvenient for content retrieval and reading.

Moreover, the existing search functions are dominated by simple retrieval, without advanced search functions. It is obvious that advanced search methods would better meet users' needs – this remains a challenge for China's OA journals.

The same statement can be made for another web service, i.e. the online submission of papers. The number of OA journals with online submission is increasing steadily but again, too many journals are still not able to provide this functionality, especially those with older information systems and platforms.

More back files

More and more OA journals are providing older content that was published five, ten or more years ago. Also, the average age of these back files is steadily increasing, with more than 100 journals providing articles more than 30 years old. Even if the majority of the available full-text has been published more recently, during the last five years or so, our survey shows that Chinese OA journals made (and continue to make) significant efforts to transform older print content with limited dissemination into digital files and to make this content available to a larger community via OA. Thus, the OA movement has had a profound influence on China's scientific and technical journals, greatly promoting the open access of the journals.

However, OA journals should continue to make efforts to increase OA to papers published before 2000, especially in social sciences and humanities where relatively few titles have digitized their archives so far.

Regarding full-text delivery, more than half of all OA journals lag behind the printed version. OA journals with preprint and current content, i.e. with instant updating at the same time as the print version, represent only 49%. The situation is improving but more work needs to be done, especially for those journals with a delay of three issues or more. OA journals with their own independent websites had a higher rate of updating than those with other online systems. Therefore, the development and construction of independent websites for OA journals should be emphasized to achieve timely updates.

Eight strategies for OA journal development

Building a suitable environment for OA journals

The further and rapid development of OA journals needs appropriate conditions. The government should maintain its favorable and encouraging attitude, creating an environment suitable for the development of OA journals and supporting them on the level of policy. Under the influence of the Chinese publishing model, the development of OA journals is limited. Therefore, the relevant departments and agencies should effectively change the journal publication system, such as running mechanisms, management systems, operation modes, approval systems and business models, and draw on the successful experience of foreign countries in order to adapt to the specific requirement of OA journals.

Enhancing the websites

The survey shows that many OA journals still lack search functionality, that these functions are often more or less basic and that the development of advanced search functions progresses (too) slowly. Moreover, less than half of OA journals support online submission, which greatly limits the development of OA journals' networking and hinders academic exchange activities. Paperless web publishing forms and online submission can accelerate the speed of academic journal publication, reduce costs, enhance international exposure and expand the influence of journals. Thus, the quality and performance of OA journals' websites needs further improvement. In addition, users are increasingly concerned about a wide range of subjective needs; therefore, the usability and aesthetics of OA journals' websites' operating systems and platforms should be guaranteed, an undertaking which requires technical support.

Developing networks

The survey also shows that the network construction of China's OA journals in general is still in its infancy, and some sites contain incomplete information and empty links. Although the statistics of all aspects have more or less improved with time, the situation does not meet the requirements of users in the information age. The construction of OA journals' networks needs to improve, especially in social sciences and in the humanities where the transition to OA dissemination of journals and the timeliness of publishing academic papers will contribute to the development of the different disciplines.

Handling the relationship with print journals

Compared to traditional printed journals, OA journals are characterized by accessibility, free use, digitized content and networking (Wang 2005). Therefore, academic communities generally consider OA journals the future of academic journals. OA journals need networking to improve dissemination, visibility and impact, in particular on the international level where their free availability gives them a real advantage compared to print journals.

However, this does not mean that print journals can exit the stage of history. Print journals have other advantages which cannot be replaced by electronic journals, such as strong stability, easy production, relatively low technical requirements, meeting most people's reading habits and few health effects on readers. Currently, traditional print journals are still highly profitable for the publishing industry, and it seems unrealistic to think that they will be completely replaced by electronic journals in the near future.

Therefore, China should handle the relationship between OA journals and print journals correctly, and ensure the interests of all parties at best, achieving the objective of co-existence and mutual assistance for both publishing formats.

Controlling the quality of papers

The article is the basic element of journals and the quality of papers is directly related to the journals' quality. The quality of papers is an important part of the Chinese evaluation of printed journals. Because China's OA journals are still mainly derived versions, their quality today depends largely on the quality of the underlying print journals. In the future, in order to ensure the simultaneous development of the quality of OA journals, authors and reviewers should be very careful about the quality of submitted papers and selection rates.

Rewarding OA journals development

The development of OA journals needs academic staff, publication agencies and technical personnel. The motivation and enthusiasm of staff and institutions is a direct correlate of the success of OA journals. Consideration and rewarding of staff and institutions play a significant role in promoting the enthusiasm of workers. Therefore, work performance related to OA journals should be included in the recent evaluation system for human resources and agencies to enhance the overall number of OA journals and to generalize their development.

Fostering balanced development in disciplines and regions

At present, the open access of China's journals is still at an early stage. OA journals are mainly in medical and life sciences, engineering and technical disciplines, while OA journals in social sciences and humanities are under-represented. Therefore, the journals in these disciplines should be supported so that they can move to OA.

Also, for economic reasons, the distribution of China's OA journals shows significant regional differences, which is not helpful for sharing and exchanging knowledge. Thus, the government and academia should take effective measures to reduce regional inequalities by mutual assistance and funding. At the same time, the authorities should provide necessary financial, technical and knowledge support to reduce the gap between rich and poor regions and to facilitate a balanced development of China's OA journals.

Protecting intellectual property

China should guarantee the intellectual property of the authors more effectively. Up to now, the copyright of Chinese papers has been largely controlled by journal publishers, with preference for print editions because of economic benefits.

In the future, in order to promote the development of OA journals, China needs to settle an agreement with publishers on the requirements and range of OA journals and to obtain written permission to reduce the resistance to digital journals and to prevent legal issues on intellectual property and piracy.

REFERENCES

Chen, MJ et al. 2011, 'Visual study of China OA journals', *Library and Information Service*, vol. 55, no. 22, pp. 133-137.

Chen, WL & Chen, RH 2013, 'Comparative analysis of three open access journal integrated content platforms', *Library Science Research*, vol. 1, no. 15, pp. 64-67.

Cheng, WH & Ren, SL 2007. 'Situation of open access publishing for Chinese scientific journals', *Acta Editologica*, vol. 19, no. 3, pp. 196-198.

Cheng, WH & Ren, SL 2008, 'Evolution of open access publishing in Chinese scientific journals', *Learned Publishing*, vol. 21, no. 2, pp. 140-152.

Cheng, WH et al. 2008, 'Situation of open access publishing for journals sponsored by the China Association for Science and Technology', *Chinese Journal of Scientific and Technical Periodicals*, vol. 19, no. 4, pp. 554-560.

Cheng, WH et al. 2009, 'Open access platforms of scientific and technical journals in foreign countries', *Chinese Journal of Scientific and Technical Periodicals*, vol. 20, no. 1, pp. 36-43.

Cheng, WH et al. 2010, 'The present state and future development of open access publishing for journals sponsored by the China Association for Science and Technology', *Science & Technology Review*, vol. 28, no. 12, pp. 19-25.

CAST 2008, *Development report of scientific and technological journals sponsored by China Association for Science and Technology*, China Scientific Press, Beijing.

CAST 2009, *Development report of scientific and technological journals sponsored by China Association for Science and Technology*, China Scientific Press, Beijing.

CAST 2010, *Development report of scientific and technological journals sponsored by China Association for Science and Technology*, China Scientific Press, Beijing.

CAST 2011, *Development report of scientific and technological journals sponsored by China Association for Science and Technology*, China Scientific Press, Beijing.

CAST 2012, *Development report of scientific and technological journals sponsored by China Association for Science and Technology*, China Scientific Press, Beijing.

Cui, LF 2013, 'Ideals and practice–the future development of OA journals', *Modern Information*, no. 3, pp. 33-39.

Geng, B & Huang, JX 2010, 'Investigation on open access publishing for university journals in China', *Chinese Journal of Scientific and Technical Periodicals*, vol. 21, no. 1, pp. 41-44.

Jin, X et al. 2012, 'An investigation on Chinese OA journals influence', *Publishing Research*, no. 10, pp. 74-78.

Qu, ZH and Shi, L 2014, 'Empirical analysis on the influencing factors on researchers accepting OA journals', *Journal of Academic Library and Information Science*, vol. 32, no. 2, pp. 5-9.

Shen, B et al. 2008, 'Investigation on open access publishing for university journals in China', *Science-Technology & Publication*, no. 11, pp. 52-54.

Wang, GQ 2005, 'OA journal–the sage in the scholarly publication field', *Modern Information*, no. 10, pp. 94-95.

Zhang, SB 2010, 'Survey and analysis on the open access journals of computer science and technology in China', *Journal of Henan Institute of Science and Technology* (Social Sciences Edition), no. 7, pp. 127-129.

Zhang, W & Pan, W 2010, 'The research in the status quo and developing strategy of OA for Chinese scientific and technology journals', *Digital Library Forum*, vol. 79, no. 12, pp. 56-60.

All websites accessed between May and July 2014.

Facts & Figures:
South Africa

Country and Economy

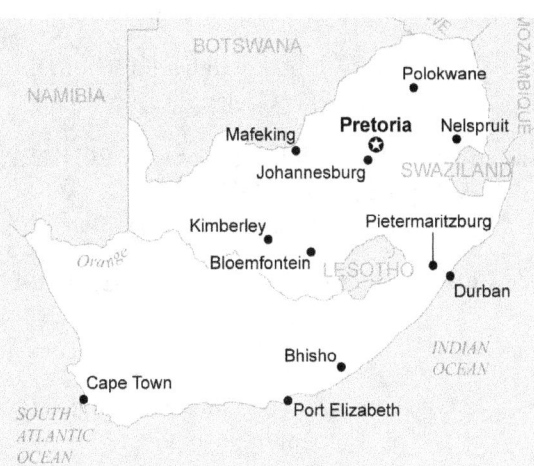

Capital	Name of Capital: Pretoria
Area	In km^2: 1,221,037
Population Size	2013 Estimate: 52,981,991 Country Ranking: 25
Density	Per km^2: 43
GDP (nominal)	In Billions of US$ (2014 estimate): 623,201 Country Ranking: 25
GDP per Capita	In US$ (2014 estimate): 11,913 Country Ranking: 71
Human Development Index	HDI (2012): 0.629 Country Ranking: 21

Research and Open Access

Scientists	Total Number (2009) (in thousand): 40.8 Per Capita: 802 per 1 million
Expenditures on Research and Development	In Billions of US$ (2011): 3.7 % of GDP: 0.7% Country Ranking: 30
Publications	Total Number (2013): 15,181 Country Ranking: 34 Number of Citable Documents: 14,180
Citations	Total Number (2013): 8,224 Country Ranking: 33 Citations per Document: 0.54 H-Index: 260
Journals	Total Number of Academic and Scholarly Journals (2014): 386 Journals with Impact Factor (2012): 50
Open Archives	Institutional Repositories: 26 Disciplinary Repositories: 2 Aggregating Repositories: 1 Governmental Repositories: 0
Open Access Journals	Total Number of Open Access Journals • UlrichsWeb: 133 • DOAJ: 70

Overview

Our last chapter is dedicated to South Africa, the young rainbow nation, the first political and military power in Africa and the last country to join the BRICS. South Africa may not have the same global influence as China or Russia but it nonetheless plays a significant role on the African continent and in particular in the Sub-Saharan region.

South Africa was one of the early adopters of the open access movement in Africa, not only because of its relatively strong culture of research production and a strong information technology infrastructure but also because of its specific tradition of sharing and common goods. As adopters of open access, South African researchers have been given a platform to freely share their scholarly output with the rest of the continent and the developing world. This option of freely sharing, which underpins the open access movement, translates into a wider distribution of published research thus presenting a model that allows free access (and often more liberal licensing terms) to publications.

The African philosophy of *Ubuntu*, which stands for a universal bond of sharing that connects all humanity, fosters and reinforces the obligation to share scholarly literature. Scientists and society are connected, and the distribution of scholarly literature must contribute to the growth and development of research and society. Such interconnectedness points to the fact that the research process is only complete when the end product in the form of scholarly output is read: hence the importance of its wide distribution.

According to the authors, open access also contributes to reversing the unidirectional information flow from the global North to the global South, as knowledge produced in the global South can now become available via open access platforms to the global North, thus improving the visibility of the former and increasing its usage and impact. At the same time, open access enhances the protection and preservation of local knowledge by having it captured and digitized and made available to an international audience.

These and other aspects make this chapter more political than the rest of the book. And it raises some crucial questions, such as the impact on other countries and learning not from the Western hemisphere or the global North but from other emerging countries such as India (publishing industry) and Brazil (launch of SciELO-

SA). Another question is about the underlying philosophy of open access. It is generally accepted (see our introduction) that open access has to do with open society and open science, as defined by Karl Popper and promoted by Georges Soros. But does it, really? The case of Russia already showed how the open access movement could be fed by other socialist traditions. Here, in South Africa, the roots of open access appear to be even stronger and deeper in the culture and philosophy of African humanism.

The last point is on protection. Generally, protection means hiding, banning access and raising barriers. How can open access help to protect local content? The authors explain how, especially via institutional and other open repositories.

About the Authors

Reggie Raju is the Deputy Director of the University of Cape Town Libraries. Until 2013, he was Director of the Client Services, Library and Information Service, at Stellenbosch University. He has been in academic libraries for more than 25 years. Reggie Raju served on the Executive Committee of the LIS professional association in South Africa (LIASA). He is currently on the Editorial Management Team of the *South African Journal of Libraries and Information Science* and on the Editorial Board of *Perspectives in International Librarianship*. He holds a PhD in Library and Information Sciences. He is the author of several publications in peer-reviewed journals, chapters in books and a book publication. He has published and presented nationally and internationally on the issue of open access. Reggie Raju is currently a member of the Academic and Research Libraries Standing Committee of IFLA.

Jaya Raju is Associate Professor and Head of the Library and Information Studies Centre at the University of Cape Town. She is also an Honorary Associate Professor in the Information Studies Programme at the University of KwaZulu-Natal. Jaya Raju has served on the Editorial Advisory Board of the *South African Journal of Libraries and Information Science* since 2005 and is currently the Editor-in-Chief of the journal. She also serves on the Editorial Advisory Board of the *Journal for Gender, Information and Development in Africa*. She has published numerous papers in peer-reviewed national and international journals and has also presented papers at local, national and international conferences (including peer-reviewed conference papers). Jaya Raju is an NRF rated researcher.

Ina Smith is the Scholarly Communications Manager at Stellenbosch University. She has been in academic libraries for 22 years. Ina Smith has actively worked with institutional repositories and open access publishing, and published and presented nationally and internationally on the issue of open access and related topics. During 2013 UNESCO entrusted her with the task of co-authoring an online curriculum on open access. Her work was acknowledged by the Electronic Publishing Trust during 2012 for highly significant contributions to the progress of global and open access to knowledge, covering the areas of advocacy, OA journals and OA repositories, training, best-practice and support.

South Africa: the role of open access in promoting local content, increasing its usage and impact and protecting it

Reggie Raju, Jaya Raju and Ina Smith

Introduction

The open access (OA) movement began to gain momentum in Africa in the mid-2000s with South Africa being one of the early adopters. South Africa's relatively strong culture of research production and a strong information technology infrastructure had significant influence in determining the path of this adoption. As adopters of open access, South African researchers have been given a platform to freely share their scholarly output with the rest of the continent and the developing world. This option of freely sharing, which underpins the open access movement, translates into wider distribution of published research thus presenting a model that allows free access (and often more liberal licensing terms) to publications.

Like most other countries, South Africa ventured down the open access path through the adoption of institutional repositories (IRs) which allowed institutions to share their research output freely online. As the norm, an IR is developed at an organization, usually a university, and is frequently run by the university's library. Populating the repository is influenced by policies or practices encouraging or requiring open access depositing. It is these policies or practices that have emerged to be significant contributors to stimulating the open access movement. However, given the relative status of newcomers to the open access movement, policies or guidelines phrased as 'requests' or 'encouragement' are used as stepping stones to mandatory open access policies. Motivations for the development of mandatory open access policies center on increasing access and usage of information and improving the impact of research findings. Other significant motivators are the protection of local content and fulfilling the requirements of funded research. One of the key arguments for open access to publicly funded research is precisely that it has been funded by the public, who should not have to pay again to view the results.

These motivations for open access align with the views of Joseph (2012) who asserts that open access plays a strong role in the foundation for research, emphasizing that OA provides the "most efficient ways to communicate results and amplifying [sic] all of its desired outcomes: accelerating discoveries, fostering innovation, creating new business opportunities, and contributing to the welfare of society as a whole".

Open Access and the African philosophy of "Ubuntu"

There is no doubt that South Africa has a significant role to play in advocating for openly sharing scholarly literature for the growth and development of the country and the continent. The principles of open access resonate well with the African philosophy of *Ubuntu*. The synergy between open access and *Ubuntu* is underscored by the innate principle of sharing. *Ubuntu* is a southern African term that brings to the fore socialism or humanism – it highlights the fact that one cannot exist as a human being in isolation (Chaplin 2006). There is a sense of interconnectedness with generosity being at the core. The spirit of *Ubuntu* is aptly captured by famous anti-apartheid cleric Desmond Tutu: "We think of ourselves far too frequently as just individuals, separated from one another, whereas you are connected and what you do affects the whole world. When you do well, it spreads out; it is for the whole of humanity".

Open access promotes the distribution of scholarly literature for the growth and development of research and society–connecting researcher, society and development. The issue of connectedness highlights the fact that the research process is only complete when the end product is distributed as widely as possible. In this globally connected information society, the researcher is both the user and creator of information or knowledge as access to current information is critical for the production of new knowledge. Hence open access becomes critical both at the beginning and at the end of the research cycle – from the conceptualization of the research problem to the distribution of the research findings. This is particularly relevant in the African context where poor access to scholarly content has negatively impacted research output emanating from Africa, relegating Africa to the periphery of world knowledge production. To corroborate the above assertion, reference is made to an earlier publication by Raju et al. (2013) who point out that "despite the desperate need for trusted and relevant information for African development, Nwagwu & Ahmed (2009) make the point that sub-Saharan Africa has not made any significant contribution to the world's research output. In fact, Africa has supplied only 0.7% of the output with a very large percentage of that coming from South Africa. This statistic may well be a true reflection of scientific activities in Africa, however, there is sufficient evidence to suggest that the low profile of scientists in Africa is attributed to poor access to scientific publications" (p.45-46). Hence it is incumbent upon South African researchers and research institutions to contribute to bridging the 'research-exchange divide' between the global South and North through the adoption of open access practices and policies that enhance sharing of scholarly output for the generation of new knowledge.

OPEN ACCESS, BASIC HUMAN RIGHTS AND SOCIAL JUSTICE

Building on the above idea about South Africa leading the open access movement on the African continent, the authors in this section examine, albeit briefly, the influence of politics and the fight for social justice on open access. McKinley (2003) makes the point that the political, social and economic structure of the apartheid system in South Africa was built on the foundation of an institutionalized violation of basic human rights. McKinley asserts that the "entire struggle against apartheid was fundamentally, a struggle for the democratic reclamation of those human rights, whether civil and political, socio-economic and/or environmental, cultural and developmental rights. It was the popular strength and depth of this struggle that succeeded in bringing an end to the apartheid system and that ushered in the formal democratic victory in 1994".

Gray & Wiens (2012) bring to the fore the connection between the open access movement and access to information, and the fight for democracy and basic human rights. They make the assertion that the values enshrined in the open access movement in South Africa are reflected in the history of the anti-apartheid struggle, from the 1955 Freedom Charter with its affirmation of learning and access to books as essential aspects of a democratic society to the 1996 constitution, which has clear provisions for access to information and education. The Soweto students' uprising of 1976 brought educational issues to the heart of the liberation movement.

South Africa's constitution is hailed as one of the most progressive in the world and the one right contained in the Constitution that symbiotically connects all other rights is the right of access to information. Affirming this symbiotic connection, the Open Democracy Advice Centre (2011) cites Article 19 of the Universal Declaration of Human Rights which states that everyone has the right to freedom of opinion and expression; this right includes freedom to hold opinions without interference and to seek, receive and impart information and ideas through any media and regardless of frontiers[1]. Expanding on the freedom of opinion and expression and linking this to improved access to information, the Committee on Economic, Social and Cultural Rights (2005) also cites the Universal Declaration of Human Rights which states that everyone has the right to the protection of the moral and material interests resulting from any scientific, literary or artistic production[2].

The Open Democracy Advice Centre (2011) goes on to claim that the right to information forms part of human rights and freedoms, and it is essential to be able to access information from public authorities in order to exercise individual human rights and freedoms. This is particularly true for disadvantaged groups, and especially in a country

---

1   Right to access information: training manual. http://www.r2k.org.za/wp-content/uploads/.../rti-training-manual-dec-2012.pdf

2   Thirty-fifth session. Geneva, 7-25 November 2005 http://www1.umn.edu/humanrts/gencomm/escgencom17.html

where information does not ordinarily flow freely. Drawing from the claims of the Centre, the authors propose that access to information must be broader than just including information held by government and must include all publicly funded research. Such proposals are not unique as Adi Kamdar argues "that it's hard to believe that we are still arguing about open access to publicly funded research. The issue is as clear as it gets: we paid for the research; most researchers are devoted, by nature and profession, to sharing their work; and the public benefits of open access can be tremendous"[3]. Further, Nicholson (2011), in pursuing some return on investment, demands that peer-reviewed research outputs be made freely available in full to the public via an open access platform, at the earliest possible date. Major funding organizations such as the European Commission, Wellcome Trust, the U.S. National Institute of Health and the Australian Research Council see open access as a public good and view it as being critical for social justice and as being a bastion for democracy and a knowledge society (Gray & Wiens 2012).

It is beyond debate that access to information is essential to uphold basic human rights and to promote social justice. Bowdoin (2011) makes the assertion that individuals and organizations across the globe recognize the need for access to information to redress local and global social inequalities. The open access movement is acknowledged as the movement to redress the access to information imbalance and to aid in the equalization of the flow of information between industrialized and less industrialized nations. Willinsky (2006) draws attention to the fact that OA extends the research capacities of developing nations, increasing public rights of access to knowledge, and furthering the policy and political contributions of research. Open access, as pronounced by Ahmed (2007), is a means of eliminating the factors that inhibit the flow of knowledge from the global South to the North and vice versa. If embraced, the movement is likely to expose the true level of scientific activities going on in Africa and other developing regions as well as give these regions access to those sources that have been hitherto inaccessible to them.

---

3   Kamdar, A. 2014. In the open access fight, big publishers are the biggest hurdle. https://www.eff.org/deeplinks/2014/01/open-access-fight-big-publishers-are-biggest-hurdle

While OA journals can aid in rectifying the imbalances of information flows from North to South, they cannot make a substantial impact on reversing information flows unless the journals are made radically accessible. It is argued that African researchers are more likely to identify relevant literature using indexing tools such as Google Scholar and other free search engines: "Today's researchers ... are likely to search Google before any other resource. So, if they are not on Google, they don't exist!" (Nicholson 2011). Such 'indexing mechanisms' will aid in the South to South flow of information. Given that many scholars in industrialized nations are also becoming frequent users of Google Scholar, the flow of scholarly information from South to North is hence enhanced (Ouya 2006).

This freer flow of information from South to South, North to South and South to North dispels the acceptance of one-way flow of information (that is, North to South). Further, this freer flow begins to lay a foundation for a more equitable flow of information and a reversal of straight North to South distribution. Another benefit of this freer flow of information, as proposed by Raju et al. (2013), is the repositioning of Africa from the periphery of knowledge production to its epicenter.

The South African research landscape and open access

The South African higher education environment was re-landscaped in 2000 to re-dress, *inter alia*, an apartheid higher educational system. The re-landscaping also targeted widening access to tertiary education. In the process, the 36 public higher education institutions were reconfigured to create 23 institutions. Smaller universities and technikons (vocationally focused, technology oriented higher education institutions) were merged to form new entities, including traditional universities, universities of technology and comprehensive universities. Six comprehensive universities were created to offer a combination of academic and vocational diplomas and degrees. The Universities of Technology (UoTs), of which there are six, focus on vocationally oriented education and offer, in the main, diplomas. The remaining eleven institutions are traditional universities offering theoretically oriented university degrees. Over and above these 23 institutions, there are three other institutions in South Africa that have a significant commitment to research production and these are the South African Medical Research Council, the Human Sciences Research Council and the Council for Scientific and Industrial Research.

It is against this background that this chapter examines open access in South Africa. The commitment to open access is in many ways influenced by the status of the institution. The academic remit of a UoT is to deliver vocationally oriented education, and hence the focus on research production, in most cases, is secondary. By default, research output is relatively low. By the same token, there is a high expectation of substantial research output from traditional universities as one of the core goals of these institutions is research production. The same, that is, high research output, is expected from the research councils. Comprehensive universities are considered more 'middle of the road' with commensurate expectations of research output. Given the core responsibilities, in terms of research output, associated with the different categories of institutions, it would be fair to expect traditional universities and research councils to invest substantially in open access for the sharing of research output.

INSTITUTIONAL REPOSITORIES

Institutional repositories, as indicated by Lynch (2003), were first developed as an online solution for collecting, preserving, and disseminating the scholarship of universities, colleges, and other research institutions. The repository quickly evolved into a platform for libraries to publish and showcase the entire breadth of an institution's scholarship including articles, books, theses, dissertations, and journals. Added support for images, video, audio, and other media has brought greater depth to repository collections. Since 2000, a number of repository platforms have been developed, each with their own set of benefits and technical criteria.

Initially it was believed that repositories had to be open source and locally installed. The open source platforms offered unlimited flexibility for developers to build custom features and collections. However, over the past decade, the platforms have been enhanced to include many of the features that would previously have required local customization. Additionally, the potential high cost of ongoing development and maintenance of locally-hosted software has led many institutions to move to hosted options. The fear of lock-in associated with specific solutions has also faded due to the success of interoperability tools, such as OAI-PMH, available on each of the platforms. IR managers, sometimes on their second or third IR platform, can attest to the relative ease with which one can move from one platform to another (Bankier & Gleason 2014).

Significance of promoting access

Open access benefits researchers, institutions, nations and society as a whole. For researchers, it brings immediate visibility of research output and increased usage of their work as open access explicitly removes *price barriers* (such as subscriptions, licensing fees, pay-per-view fees) and *permission barriers* (such as most copyright and licensing restrictions) for the end user. Further, there is sufficient evidence to show that open access increases the impact factor for the researcher (Raju et al. 2012, Jeffrey 2006). Institutions enjoy the same benefits in aggregated form, including an elevation of its status per the various ranking systems. Ezema (2013) sums-up the benefits of open access for universities in developing countries when he points out that research generated in developing countries are poorly disseminated and therefore lack global visibility. The publication of these research findings in institutional repositories at individual universities will not only improve the visibility and utilization of the research but will also increase the global ranking of the universities and researchers who have published their research in the repository.

If one extrapolates the benefits of open access to the level of a country, there is growing evidence to show that the country of the researcher also benefits as it increases the impact of the research on the citizenry of the country. In effect, there will be a better return on investment for publicly funded research. Society as a whole benefits as the research is more accessible to the tax paying citizenry and, especially in developing countries, a stimulus for growth and development (Jain 2012, Ezema 2013). Substantiating this view is the Nature Publishing Group (2014) which points out that the proponents of open access argue that there is a benefit for society in general, and in doing so it cites the UK's Wellcome Trust: "the benefits of research are derived principally from access to research results", and therefore "society as a whole is made worse off if access to scientific research results is restricted"[4].

---

4   The pros and cons of open access. http://www.nature.com/nature/focus/accessdebate/34.html#b

In this age of ubiquitous access to information enabled by the World Wide Web, it is possible for research findings to be disseminated free of charge to anyone who wishes to read them. Given this ubiquitous nature of information, access to scholarly journals is quicker and easier in the case of open access content. As alluded to above, access is enhanced through robust search engine capabilities such as Google which can quickly track down the open access literature hosted by institutional and subject repositories.

The freedom to publish enhances usage of content in repositories of developing countries thus providing the rest of the world with outputs from scholars who previously had difficulty publishing in journals in the developed world. The challenges of publishing in 'western' journals, poor research infrastructure, poor funding opportunities and such, has fuelled the brain drain from developing parts of the world such as Africa.

From brain drain to brain gain: the role of open access

There is significant evidence in the literature confirming that Africa (and South Africa is not exempt) suffers from an acute case of 'brain drain' to wealthier countries such as Australia, Canada, the USA, and the United Kingdom who have strong research infrastructures. Exacerbating this brain drain is the fact that knowledge generated from and on the continent is not readily accessible to potential users on the continent. In the brain drain process, the physical migration of researchers is viewed as 'hard brain drain' and the unavailability of research results to users is viewed as 'soft brain drain' (Geber 2013). The 'hard brain drain' factors which attract Africans to other countries include, *inter alia*, poor research infrastructure including poor access to scholarly information to support research output (Weinberg 2011, Geber 2013).

The open access movement aids and abets in stemming the 'soft brain drain' by providing a conduit that improves the availability and accessibility of African research generated by African scholars through websites and via African universities actively participating in open access practices. The growth of African open access journals is on the rise. The South African research environment is in a very strong position to reverse the 'brain drain' process. It needs to strive to emulate the Indian example which shows a net inflow of scientists and concomitant elevated outflow of research output. The Indians have shown that productivity of incoming and visiting scientists are higher than that of the average staying and outgoing scientist. India has reversed the 'brain drain' and is marching towards a 'brain gain'. The South African open access strategy has the capacity to showcase the research output of the country, its research niche areas and its areas of research excellence.

South Africa is ideally placed to develop a roadmap for its own version of the 'brain gain' because it has a growing research infrastructure, the technology to support the infrastructure, and the 'raw material/data' for new research areas and innovation. The improved visibility of research output, through constructive exploitation of the open access movement, has the capacity to attract research collaboration opportunities and high caliber postgraduate research students. Lucrative funding or grants resulting from improved visibility of research output, improved collaboration opportunities and higher caliber of international postgraduate students will attract research leaders – including both returning South Africans and foreign scientists. The upsurge of South Africa's research agenda is reliant on open and free access to scholarly research.

As indicated by Joseph (2012), faster, barrier-free access to scholarly literature will allow users to identify, extract, and incorporate new ideas from the literature and data more rapidly into product development cycles. Joseph reports that "this is already speeding innovation in industries such as biotechnology, where models of openly sharing data are being experimented with in the drug development process, potentially shortening the time from development to market for effective new treatments and therapies". This high speed translation of ideas into innovative new services, products, and other commercial ventures is likely to fuel the 'brain gain' and hence economic growth in South Africa.

Staying with the theme of connectedness, one of the inherent strengths of open access is that it offers a genuine opportunity to democratize access to a critical layer of information, and to open channels for communication and collaboration between/among scholars who previously would never have had the chance to connect. The JISC Report on open access, drafted by Parsons et al. (2011), also clears the misnomer that scholarly literature is for the higher education sector only. The report demonstrates the significant benefit of open access to the public sector flowing from connecting the public to that critical layer of information that makes it an informed society. Open access offers the rank and file of society the opportunity to be active participants in the scholarly and research process. Far from simply enabling interested members of the public, anywhere and anytime, to access and consume information, open access enables them to actively contribute to the generation of knowledge.

Impact

To reiterate, open access is a significant medium for connecting the researcher, as user and creator, and society to scholarly information. The sense of sharing of scholarly information has complimentary spinoffs as researchers, seeking outlets for their publications, pursue avenues that maximize citation for their research. Davis et al. (2008), in reinforcing the link between open access and improved citation counts, state that citations provide stable links to cited documents and make a public statement of intellectual recognition for the cited authors. Citations are an indicator of the dissemination of an article in the scientific community and provide a quantitative system for public recognition of work by qualified peers.

Having work cited is therefore an incentive for scholars. To demonstrate the synergy between open access and citation counts, Davis et al. (2008) go on to point out that freely available online research generates more than three times the average number of citations received by print articles. The primary explanation offered for the citation advantage of open access articles is that freely available articles are cited more because they are read more than their subscription-only counterparts. Corroborating their assertions, Antelman (2004) reports that open access articles have a greater research impact than articles that are not freely available and opines that this finding will reinforce librarians' commitment to the open access agenda including negotiating rights with publishers. Further, as custodians of institutional repositories, librarians are influencing the development of alternative metrics.

In the current scholarly environment, journal-level impact is the norm as opposed to the evaluation of authors of individual articles. It is a given that journal impact factors correlate poorly with actual citations of individual articles. Therefore, in an environment that promotes the ingestion of individual articles in repositories, it becomes increasingly important to measure the impact of individual articles, and hence a demand for new citation measures. Open access articles and new citation measures provide this meaningful method of measuring the impact of research. This assertion is supported by Cullen and Chawner (2011) who point out that open access content is more citable, not because of the quality of the output but rather because of the advantage that open access brings in maximizing accessibility, and thereby improving citability. They go on to demonstrate, via research conducted, that open access will enhance the research community's existing system for evaluating and rewarding research productivity. Nicholson (2011) reiterates this assertion by maintaining that open access radically enhances international visibility and accessibility of scholarly works. If works are not accessible, they will not be read. If they are not read, they will not be cited. If they are not cited, the implication is the work does not have impact nor does it have scholarly reputation.

In response to the demand to source an alternative to the widely used journal impact factor and personal citation indices like the h-index, the open access movement has brought to the fore altmetrics. This alternative metrics measures article level impact. Further, it measures more than just citation counts, but also other aspects of the impact of a work, such as how many data and knowledge bases refer to it, article views, download, or mentions in social media and news media. The rapid evolution of bibliometrics toward 'webometrics', 'cybermetrics' and 'influmetrics', brings new citation measurement tools to the fore.

Paradox in open access

The issue of the paradox within open access in developing countries, including South Africa, begins with statements such as that by Vaughn Cooper[5]: "I do not wish to contribute to the [access] problem by publishing in journals that my colleagues at institutions with limited libraries, or readers with no academic libraries whatsoever, cannot access". At the same time, young researchers seeking to establish themselves as researchers aspire to publish in 'high-impact' journals which more often than not are not open access at this point

---

5   Cooper, V. 2014. The Paradox of Open Access. http://mikethemadbiologist.com/2014/06/01/the-paradox-of-open-access

in time. The cost of publishing in hybrid 'high-impact' journals, via author processing charges which enables open access publishing at a fee, is way beyond the affordability of these young researchers. Hence the paradox.

As indicated, the primary purpose of open access is to improve access to the end user. Young African researchers, as authors, are skeptical of open access; however, they are dependent on open access for access to scholarly information to support their research. The skepticism is fuelled by firstly, the perceived lack of value or impact of open access material, secondly, by the lack of resources to support the article charges for open access publishing and, thirdly, their advisors perhaps do not publish in open access journals, or do not recommend open access publishing. Another compelling factor is the push by smaller institutions for the visibility of publishing in well-read, 'higher impact' journals. It is argued by the smaller institutions that the larger institutions can afford to take the moral high ground with regard to open access as they have higher 'traffic' of research output, have a larger number of leading researchers visiting their institutions, and are not terribly challenged in attracting grants and collaboration and in developing collegial networks.

For Africa, South Africa and young researchers, the very best open access publications must recruit and promote articles from authors from 'smaller' institutions, waive open access fees and devote editorial services to provide visibility. Also, these authors need access to scholarly literature to produce research and to be empowered to distribute that research to fellow Africans and young researchers. Access to local content (elaborated on in the next section) is critical for the generation of new knowledge and to move Africa from the periphery of world knowledge production to the epicenter: to move Africa from being a pure consumer of knowledge to being a producer of knowledge.

Protection and preservation of local content

It is important, for the promotion of the usage of local content and for its protection, that there is support from respective principals for open access policies. Further, support and guidance from national governments and major funders are imperative. It is common cause that policies are important for motivating researchers to publish in open access systems. It is also important for clarifying objectives, processes and procedures relating to open access activities.

Kaniki & Mphahlele (2002) highlight the need to protect local knowledge by capturing and digitizing it and then making it available to the international audience. They make the assertion that "knowledge produced by universities and research institutes around the world is gathered, documented and disseminated in a coherent way (...) the same should be done with community-based, local or indigenous knowledge (...) It should be included, alongside the more usual scientific knowledge, as part of national and international discussions and development and the strengthening of intellectual capacity".

This need to protect local knowledge must be examined in the context of what Bappa (2012) claims to be the vulnerability of African traditional knowledge; African local content is being systematically undermined and erased by the invasion of news and information from other cultures, particularly those of 'the West', which reaches the population through the global media. Owusu-Ansah & Mji (2013), writing from an Afrocentric paradigm, highlight the need to promote local content and knowledge. They argue for the need for an emancipatory and participatory type of research system which values and includes local content and knowledge. In the predominantly western-oriented academic circles and investigations, the African voice is either sidelined or suppressed because local knowledge and methods are often ignored or not taken seriously. They go on to argue that African-based research must include African thought and ideas from inception through to completion and to the implementation of innovation arising from the research. In this way the research is both empowering and meaningful with accurate contextualization.

This 'undermining and erasing' of local African content must be viewed in the context of a collective culture that has stood the test of time. It is enriched by its ancestral customs and a unique myriad of languages and cultures, each of which contains specific ancient knowledge, which constitute a source of precious wealth for humanity. It is enriched by its indigenous peoples and their oral culture.

Given this rich tradition, Africa must seek ways to break into the globalized world as part of society and the knowledge economy. However, it must break through via its own development path. Brewer (2014) adds that African researchers need to persist in developing and using alternative methods of studying their reality and refrain from adhering to the research pathways mapped out by western methodologies. Whilst Africa neither seeks to negate nor denigrate known western methods of investigation, its intention is to challenge researchers and African scholars in particular into alternative methods of inquiry in the investigation and preservation of local content and knowledge, for purposes of development and empowerment.

In order to carve its own path, Africa must ensure that traditional, cultural and historical knowledge is given top priority in the education system, so that its citizens have the identity they need to organize and establish their lives in the 21st century. At the same time, intellectual development in all fields, particularly science and technology, must be pursued and strengthened. The true history of Africa, which has been distorted by those who have exploited it, must be restored. Therefore, it is imperative, as pointed out by Pickover & Mohale (2013), that local knowledge be captured, digitized and distributed to the widest possible audience. Open access is the platform that will ensure the widest possible audience. The information that is made available in this open forum could be research output on these issues, as well as primary information or digitized data.

In alignment with these views, Mudzaki (2013) stresses that "given the dynamic nature of information technologies and obsolescence issue associated with them, it is important to put in place digital preservation strategy". He goes on to say that digital preservation ensures a series of managed activities for continued access to digital materials for as long as necessary, beyond the limits of media failure or technological change.

Digital preservation ensures continuity and is, for all intents and purposes, at the end of the open access process. However, it is more important to examine the preceding processes, namely, the capture and digitization of local content: contributions by Africans to history and civilization are captured, curated, disseminated and preserved. Unfortunately, in the current climate, African history and civilization is conspicuously missing from text books for formal education and generally remain unknown to other Africans and to the rest of the world. Owusu-Ansah & Mji (2013) confirm this scenario when they claim that "silenced contributions from ancient Egyptian education to philosophy, mathematics, architecture, medicine and library science are just a few" examples of local content that is conspicuously missing from main stream education. They go on to point out that "a quick review of the literature reveals that Africa has historically made a host of contributions to world civilization which remain unknown and subliminally perpetuate the myth that African societies are incapable of rigorous scientific inquiry".

This conspicuous absence of African content must be viewed in the environment of globalization and technological change that are driving new developments in electronic publishing and learning. Limb (2005) points out that the new "scramble for Africa" is for information resources to digitize which suggests a new process is unfolding, that is, the digitization of Africa. The challenge for all involved in the digitization of African resources is to ensure access, sustainability, and fairness in the sharing of these resources. Open access must be given the priority to achieve the goal of protecting local content, ensuring that it is accessible and can contribute to world knowledge. Improved access will have the domino effect of increasing usage and concomitant impact. Scholars and their institutions in the global North will benefit from the increased access to digitized data about Africa. Improved access, as stated earlier, will provide long-term solutions to the deep-seated educational and publishing crises in Africa.

Another significant issue in the drive to protect local knowledge is the 'buy-in' from respective governments. A 'government driven' process will enhance visibility and accessibility of research. South Africa is in the enviable situation, as compared to the rest of the continent, that the South African government supports research to address local issues and to share the results of that research with the rest of the continent as most of the countries on the continent share similar problems. The increase in visibility of research output will increase usage of such output to address continental problems which will demonstrate impact and return on investment on funder-supported research, including research funded by government.

SOUTH AFRICAN GOVERNMENT INSTITUTIONS AND SUPPORT FOR OPEN ACCESS

The South African government launched, on 22 July 2013, the first open access site for scholarly journals on the African continent. This site, according to Janine Erasmus[6], is the South African version of the South American Scientific Electronic Library Online. The South African version (SciELO-SA) is a searchable full-text journal database that is completely open-access, that is, free to access and free to publish. SciELO-SA is expected to strengthen the scholarly journal evaluation, editing, publishing and accreditation systems in the country, as indicated on the project's website. The SciELO-SA project is funded by the Department of Science and Technology, maintained by the Academy of Science of South Africa (ASSAf), and endorsed by the Department of Higher Education and Training.

There are "mandatory quality criteria" to become a full member which include, *inter alia*, high publishing standards, well maintained periodicity, curated and well managed data, and a title that conforms to bandwidth and intellectual property rights standards. Further, journals are only included on the SciELO-SA platform once they receive a favorable evaluation from ASSAf's journal quality peer-review panel.

There are a number of benefits for both users and producers of research output. For the user, the SciELO-SA platform is accessible for printing and sharing abstracts and full text articles. For the researcher, more than making the content accessible to the user, the site provides usage statistics based on the number of article downloads, and impact indicators based on citations – this allows tracking of not only individual journals' performance, but each journal collection as a whole. The information gathered from tracking will in turn improve the process of evaluating scholarly articles. Further, SciELO-SA provides mechanisms and/or permissions for improved dissemination such as the ability to send the article via email, or to post a link to social media platforms.

Clearly, there is commitment by the national government in South Africa to promote sharing of research output via open access. Given this commitment, it would not be presumptuous to assume that there would be commitment from institutions of higher education. Firstly, as public funded institutions it would be obligatory for South African higher education institutions to share research output. Secondly, one of the core responsibilities of higher education institutions is

---

6   Erasmus, J. 2013. Open-access research data for SA. http://mediaclub-southafrica.com/tech/3425-open-access-research-data-to-boost-science-sector

to produce research and the sharing of the research contributes to knowledge production and to the standing of the institution. Thirdly, a significant motivator for the publication of research is recognition by peers for the researcher's contribution to quality knowledge production and hence the desire to share research output with the widest possible audience.

There is significant evidence to demonstrate that South African higher education institutions have taken on, primarily via their libraries, the responsibility of providing open access services. Confirming this assertion is the claim by UNESCO that South Africa is a leading African country in terms of open access at the governmental level and in terms of grass-roots open access initiatives in universities and research organizations[7]. South African research organizations and academic institutions have joined the global drive of making knowledge available in a free and open manner. The drive within South Africa is gaining momentum as more academic institutions and research organizations begin to participate: the spirit of cooperation and sharing is the underpinning factor in the drive. However, this drive brings with it its own set of challenges. New open access services that libraries are providing or trying to provide demand a new set of skills from the librarian.

Librarians, scientists and publishers

Higher education libraries that are providing open-access services such as institutional repositories or open-access journals face several key challenges including a new skills-set (Antelman 2004). Within this open access environment, librarians need to draw on a sophisticated understanding of the scholarly communication practices of individual disciplines, even as they are rapidly evolving. Librarians need to understand scholars' use of pre-publication research material not traditionally part of the domain of libraries in a print environment. The road to rolling-out an institutional repository necessitates librarians soliciting prime research output for ingestion. Data showing that freely available articles in their discipline are more likely to be cited, is powerful evidence of the value of repositories as well as other open-

---

7   UNESCO Global open access portal http://www.unesco.org/new/en/communication-and-information/portals-and-platforms/goap/access-by-region/africa/south-africa

access channels. Hence the advocacy role of librarians in an open access environment is imperative.

Open access is still not a part of daily research practices of researchers and research administrators. Soliciting of content for open access must be viewed against the background of researchers not having the time to self-archive – it (that is, self-archiving) does not fit in with their research workflows. Researchers still need to be convinced of the benefits of open access; they perceive repositories as being in conflict with their publishers, there is confusion regarding post-print versions and post-prints are not seen as authoritative versions. The fact that open access practices are not rewarded in institutional promotion is a draw-back (Jain 2012).

A major bane for open access is copyright, publishers' restrictions and embargoes. Given that open access is predicated upon unrestricted online access to articles published in scholarly journals, books or monographs, copyright, publishers' restrictions and embargoes become significant issues. The challenges remain for repository managers on how to handle these complex issues. Self-archiving clauses are not included in national licenses for access to e-resources and IR managers have to clear rights for every deposited item. Further, many South African publishers do not have self-archiving policies.

SURVEY OF THE SOUTH AFRICAN OPEN ACCESS LANDSCAPE

A survey of the South African open access landscape conducted in June 2014 confirms the commitment of South African higher education institutions to open access. Nineteen of the 23 higher education institutions and two research councils completed a questionnaire that was administered by the authors. The questionnaires were required to be completed by the institutions' repository managers and covered the categories that follow.

Growth of repositories

Figure 5.1, extracted from OpenDOAR[8], shows the growth of repositories in South Africa between 2005 and 2014 (July 12).

---

8 http://www.opendoar.org

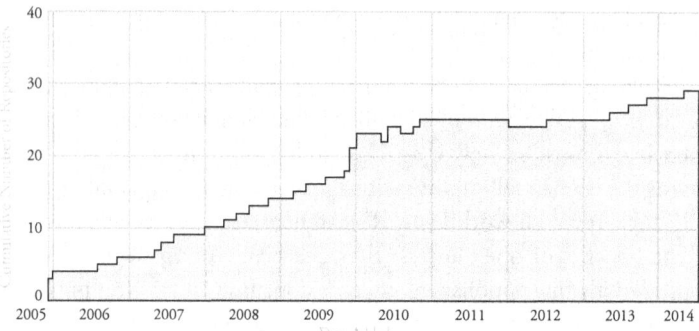

Figure 5.1: Repositories in South Africa (Source: OpenDOAR)

An examination of the growth of repositories in Africa (see Table 5.1) shows an incline while the growth of repositories in South Africa seems to have leveled-out. This is an indication that repositories in South Africa are in a maturing phase. The fact that South African repositories are in a 'maturing phase' coupled with the advantage of the country having a relatively strong research infrastructure with concomitantly high research output, places South Africa in the prime position of taking a leadership role on the continent in sharing research output.

Year	Total African repositories	South African repositories
2010	48	25
2011	51	24
2012	61	25
2013	91	28

Table 5.1: Comparative African-South Africa growth of repositories (Source: OpenDOAR)

Further, South Africa's leadership role and the potential to share via an open access platform offer the developing world unprecedented access to knowledge. However, it is also brings with it the threat that unless there is mass mobilization, mass investment in systems to protect and support the creation of research, the curation and profiling of local knowledge, the global South stands to be subsumed in a deluge of knowledge from the global North. This one-way deluge will reinforce the global digital and participation divide.

An interesting finding from the analysis of the responses to this survey is the expansion of the role and responsibility of a consortium to provide open access services. The SEALS consortium (a consortium of higher education libraries in the Eastern Cape province of South Africa) demonstrates the willingness of higher education institution libraries to collaborate in order to overcome logistical issues, such as a limited skills pool to manage IT infrastructure relating to open access. It is the opinion of the authors that there is a great deal of potential in collaboration as it eliminates the need at individual institutions for a skills pool that is still in its infancy. Further, updates to software need to be done once within the consortium on one server which can be maintained centrally and all updates can be done centrally. However, the 'centralization' of the IT does not address the issue of ingestion. Librarians at the respective institutions must be trained to assist in the ingestion into a repository, in the organization of the information and, in the dissemination of the research output. Advocacy becomes a significant component of the new role and responsibility of the librarian to grow the pool of submitters of content. Further, competencies relating to copyright, publishers' restrictions and embargoes need to be acquired.

Content size in repositories

As indicated in Table 5.1, the number of institutional repositories at higher education institutions in South Africa is at a point of saturation. However, the ingestion rate or the number of items in a repository reflects the research output of the institution. Table 5.2 shows the average number of items in the repositories of the three different types of higher education institutions and the research councils. It reflects that the traditional universities have the highest average and not the research councils. Universities of Technology (UoTs) have a much lower submission rate. This is not surprising considering that their main focus is teaching as opposed to research. It is evident from the number of items in the repositories (Table 5.2), that traditional universities are making huge strides to share their research output.

Traditional Universities	10,012
Comprehensive Universities	2,326
Universities of Technology	653
Research Councils	7,530

Table 5.2: Average number of items in repositories, per institution type (2014)

Further, closer examination of the data gathered via the questionnaire reveals that 64.2% of the total number of items in repositories in South Africa is from, arguably, the five leading research universities in South Africa (Stellenbosch University, University of Cape Town, University of KwaZulu-Natal, University of Pretoria and University of the Witwatersrand). One of these top five institutions has in its repository 37.5% of the total number of items in institutional repositories nationally. To re-iterate the issue, the leading research universities are making their output available via institutional repositories.

Job titles and new roles of the librarian

Institutional repositories are becoming the mainstream responsibility of the library. The survey shows that a number of institutions have developed roles with responsibility specifically for the institution's repository. More than 50% of the respondents had job titles that were either Repository Administrator/Manager or Scholarly Communications Manager. One can infer from the titles of the remaining respondents that the incumbents carried more than one job activity. Of these, three respondents indicated repository management to be an extension of the role and responsibility of the Systems Librarian. Acquisitions Librarian, Research Librarian, Law Librarian and Specialist: Records Management and Archival Services were the other titles indicated with responsibility for the repository. It is interesting to note that the role of the Research Librarian has been extended to include this responsibility. Raju & Schoombee (2013) point out that "in the current open access environment… research librarians guide users not only on traditional publishing practices, but also on open access publishing and the different types of usage licences for their publications. There is sufficient evidence emanating from the literature that demonstrates that research support librarians are actively providing advisory services on the different channels for publishing and dissemination of research results" (p.30-31). As indicated earlier, one of the challenges for repository managers is advising on copyright and publishers' restrictions and limitations. The expansion of the role of the Research Librarian is aligned to new trends in research support. Improving usage and impact of research output is fast becoming core to the roles of the new generation Research Librarian.

Item types in repositories

Given that repositories were built on the collection, organization and dissemination of theses and dissertations, one would have assumed that all the repositories of higher education institutions in South Africa would have theses and dissertations as part of their collections (see Table 5.3). However, there are two traditional universities and two UoTs that do not have theses and dissertations in their repositories. For obvious reasons the two research councils do not include these items. With regard to the above-mentioned four institutions, one can assume that these institutions are still paper-based (in terms of their theses and dissertations) and hence this output is not available on their repositories.

Research articles	13
Theses & dissertations	13
Chapters in books	10
Conference presentations	9
Full conference papers	9
Inaugural addresses	7
Working papers	5
Data sets and other data	4

Table 5.3: Number of repositories with item types (total number = 23)

It is interesting and encouraging to note the number of institutions that have research articles in their repositories. As indicated earlier, South Africa has a relatively strong research production culture and the sharing of this output with the rest of the country and the continent is an imperative. The hosting and preservation of other content types augurs well for the development of open access with the domino effect of improved usage and impact.

Development of open access policies

The commitment to making scholarly literature available to the widest possible audience is reflected in Table 5.4. The building blocks to open sharing of content are in existence. It would seem that institutions have policies in place but are yet to implement those policies. As is expected, research data management is still an area that needs development and so too is the development of policies for the collection and dissemination of published research output either in pre-print, post-print or the publisher's version format. Despite the fact that only 13 institutions have theses and dissertations in their repositories, there are sixteen institutions that have mandatory policies for the submission of this content type. The authors make the prediction that it would not be too long before all sixteen institutions will have theses and dissertations in their repositories.

Policy	No. of respondents
Open access research	12
Institutional research repositories (as part of the records management policy)	14
Research data management and preservation (curation of data sets)–in process	11
Theses and dissertations (mandatory submission)	16
Intellectual property (incl. copyright)	16
Archival policy (special collections) (part of the records management policy)	13

Table 5.4: Institutional policies (total number of respondents = 19)

It is also interesting to note that institutions are developing policies to address the issue of copyright. Sixteen of the institutions have policies to address copyright issues. The challenge reported earlier with regard to copyright and publishers' restrictions is being addressed through the development of policies to provide the necessary guidelines to assist the library and the librarian. Such policy intervention will assist in protecting local knowledge. The insertion of open licences will assist in improving usage and citation without prejudicing the required protection.

Respondents were asked to describe what "the most important focus of the institutional repository" was. The responses demonstrated the concomitancy of supporting policies with the focus of the institutions. Only one of the 19 respondents did not rate "To provide open access to research output and increase its visibility" as the most important aspect of their repository. "To digitally curate and preserve research output for years to come" was also ranked as very important. These responses confirm the commitment, from the higher education and research councils in South Africa, to sharing research output and to improve the visibility of the output. Improved visibility will, as indicated by Nicholson (2011), improve accessibility with the end result being a greater readership. If the scholarly research is read, it will be cited thus enhancing impact.

Article processing charges and gold open access publishing

An article processing charge (APC), also known as a publication fee, is charged to authors wishing to publish in an open access journal. The survey revealed that there are three institutions in South Africa that currently support publishing of articles in open access journals through the payment of APCs. The authors are of the opinion that the movement towards open access necessitates a change in mind-set and that institutional libraries should have, as a line item, a budget for open access support. The fact that only three institutions currently support APCs means the leadership in academic libraries needs to come to grips with changing models influencing the open access movement.

Extracted from the responses was the fact that four institutions were hosting (or acting as publisher for) open access journals. The software that is being used here is Open Journal Systems (OJS). Raju et al. (2012) in describing the implementation of OJS at Stellenbosch University point out that "the Library developed an efficient local infrastructure and developed concomitant procedures to support the publication of journals using OJS... Stellenbosch University ... launched SUN Journals which is the host to the thirteen journal titles".

The authors will use one title hosted by Stellenbosch University as an exemplar to demonstrate how open access has increased visibility, accessibility and usage, and the protection of local knowledge. The *South African Journal of Libraries and Information Science* (SAJLIS) was one of the earlier titles hosted and published by Stellenbosch University using OJS. The total number of articles in SAJLIS that are hosted on OJS is 85 and this includes digitally born articles and those that have been retrospectively digitized. In less than 24 months, the

85 articles that were available via open access had 26,887 downloads with an average download of 323 per article. This is phenomenal given that this title formerly was 'limited' to a very local readership. The 26,887 downloads are distributed among 126 countries with only 56% downloads coming from South Africa. Table 5.5 lists the 'top ten countries' and their respective percentage downloads.

South Africa	55.85
India	5.10
USA	4.84
Nigeria	3.79
UK	2.26
Kenya	2.19
Australia	1.30
Tanzania	1.12
Philippines	1.09
Malaysia	1.08

Table 5.5: Usage of SAJLIS per country (in % of total downloads)

According to the usage statistics, articles from SAJLIS have been downloaded by readers in the developed world countries, BRICS countries and countries from the African continent and the Far East. The improved visibility and accessibility of the journal increased the capacity of the editorial team to attract a high profile international editorial board. Further, the whole editorial process, that is, from the online submission of the manuscript by authors to the online review and eventual online publication has contributed significantly to developing an international panel of reviewers. The fact that the process is electronic makes the process of placing the manuscripts though a plagiarism detection process much easier. These and other interventions, enhanced by its electronic format and processes, have contributed to the improvement in the quality of the journal. The high rejection rate of almost 70% of submitted manuscripts is testimony to much improved quality. The OJS managed workflow has also ensured the timely publication of issues. Since 2012 when the journal, which was traditionally published in print format, went online and open access, its twice-yearly issue has been published on time (mid-year and year-end).

The authors are of the opinion that the significant increase in downloads demonstrates an increase in visibility and accessibility. Given that the format of SAJLIS lends itself to social media manipulation, the visibility and promotion of usage is enhanced by the journal management team (not editorial team) tweeting individual articles.

The presupposition is that an article is being downloaded to be read. The chance of an article read being cited is one hundred percent greater than an article not read. Hence, it is safe to infer that the downloads reflect potential impact – developing world content is now being accessed from any part of the world that has Internet connectivity.

Summary and conclusion

South Africa's relatively strong culture of research production and its strong information technology infrastructure make it 'almost obligatory' that it adopts the open access philosophy and engages in open access practices. The African philosophy of *Ubuntu* strengthens the obligation to share scholarly literature. This sense of obligation stems from South Africa's high research output to address, *inter alia*, African imperatives. Further, given that open access promotes the distribution of scholarly literature for the growth and development of research and society, the sense of obligation becomes heightened. In the open access continuum, the researcher (as the consumer and producer of information), society and development become interconnected. Such inter-connectedness points to the fact that the research process is only complete when the end product in the form of scholarly output is read: hence its wide distribution is important. The domino effect is enhanced impact.

The process of inter-connecting assists in stemming the one directional flow of information from the global North to the global South–perpetuating Africa's relegation to the periphery of knowledge production. In removing price and licensing barriers, open access nullifies the challenge of knowledge production being stifled through poor access to scholarly content. In the same way, knowledge produced in the global South can now become available, via open access platforms, to the global North thus improving the visibility of the former and increasing its usage and impact. In the process, open access enhances the protection and preservation of local knowledge by having it captured and digitized and made available to the international audience. Protection of local content is enhanced through wide visibility, acknowledgement and, long term curation and preservation.

Appreciating the significance of open access in improving visibility, usage and impact, and the protection of local content, South African higher education institutions have begun to engage in open access practices. The authors can confidently assert that open access has become part of the fabric of the higher education landscape in South Africa, offering the developing world unprecedented access to knowledge emanating from the country. Notwithstanding that the number of higher education institutional repositories in South Africa is almost at the point of saturation, the ingestion rate or the number of items in a repository is a reflection of the research output of the respective institutions. Content that is available in South African higher education institutional repositories include chapters in books, full conference papers as well as presentation slides, data sets, inaugural addresses, research articles, theses and dissertations, and working papers. South African higher education institutions are also pursuing publishing directly in open access journals, again to improve visibility, usage and impact of research output. There is sufficient evidence to show that publications in open access platforms do radically improve visibility, usage and impact. The example of the *South African Journal of Libraries and Information Science*, as an open access journal hosted by a South African higher education institution, is a demonstration of such improved visibility, usage and, by inference, impact. Further, it is a conduit for sharing local content with the international audience. South Africa, initially by default but increasingly by design, is playing a significant role in utilizing open access platforms to promote local content, increase its usage and its impact.

References

Ahmed, A 2007, 'Open access towards bridging the digital divide–policies and strategies for developing countries', Information Technology for Development, vol. 13, no. 4, pp. 337-361.

Antelman, K 2004, 'Do open-access articles have a greater research impact?' College & Research Libraries, vol. 65, no. 5, pp. 372-382.

Bankier, JG & Gleason, K 2014, *Institutional repository software comparison*, UNESCO, Paris.

Bappa, GD 2012, 'Africa's choice: digitise traditional knowledge or lose culture and development', in The eLearning Africa 2012 report, eds. S Isaacs & D Hollow, ICWE, Germany, pp. 18-19.

Bowdoin, NT 2011, 'Open access, African scholarly publishing, and cultural rights: an exploratory usage and accessibility study', Library Philosophy and Practice.

Brewer, JK 2014, 'Indigenous knowledge and intellectual property: drug research and development in contemporary context', Intellectual Property Rights: Open Access, vol. 2, no. 3, p. 120.

Chaplin, K 2006, 'The *Ubuntu* spirit in African communities'. Working paper.

Cullen, R & Chawner, B 2011, 'Institutional repositories, open access, and scholarly communication: a study of conflicting paradigms', The Journal of Academic Librarianship, vol. 37, no. 6, pp. 460-470.

Davis, PM et al. 2008, 'Open access publishing, article downloads, and citations: randomised controlled trial', BMJ, no. 337, pp. a568+.

Ezema, IJ 2013, 'Local contents and the development of open access institutional repositories in Nigeria University libraries: challenges, strategies and scholarly implications', Library Hi Tech, vol. 31, no. 2.

Geber, H 2013, 'Can mentoring decrease the brain drain of academics from Africa?', Procedia–Social and Behavioral Sciences, no. 93, pp. 215-220.

Gray, E & Wiens, K 2012, 'South Africa: knowledge for all', in Open access and development: journals and beyond, eds. L Chan, E Gray, & R Kahn, IDS Knowledge Services, Brighton, pp. 24-27.

Jain, P 2012, 'Promoting open access to research in academic libraries', Library Philosophy and Practice.

Jeffery, KG 2006, 'Open access: an introduction', ERCIM News no. 64, pp. 16-17.

Joseph, H 2012, 'The impact of open access on research and scholarship: reflections on the Berlin 9 Open Access Conference', College & Research Libraries News, vol. 73, no. 2, pp. 83-87.

Kaniki, AM & Mphahlele, MEK 2002, 'Indigenous knowledge for the benefit of all: can knowledge management principles be used effectively?', South African Journal of Libraries and Information Science, vol. 68, no. 1.

Limb, P 2005, 'The digitization of Africa', Africa Today vol. 52, no. 2, pp. 3-19.

Lynch, CA 2003, *Institutional repositories: essential infrastructure for scholarship in the digital age,* ARL Association of Research Libraries, Washington.

McKinley, DT 2003, *The state of access to information in South Africa',* Centre for the Study of Violence and Reconciliation, Johannesburg.

Mudzaki, FK 2013, 'Digitization prospects in developing countries: case of Zimbabwe National Archives'. Paper presented at the Association of Moving Image Archivists (AMIA) Annual General Conference, Richmond, Virginia.

Nicholson, DR 2011, 'Open access: benefits for Africa', in Panel on open access in Africa and in the Caribbean: progress and prospects. Paper presented at the 77th IFLA General Conference and Assembly, Puerto Rico.

Nwagwu, WE & Ahmed, A 2009, 'Building open access in Africa', International Journal of Technology Management, vol. 45, no. ½, pp. 82-101.

Ouya, D 2006, 'Open access survey of Africa-published journals', INASP infobrief no. 7.

Owusu-Ansah, FE & Mji, G 2013, 'African indigenous knowledge and research', African Journal of Disability, vol. 2, no. 1.

Parsons, D et al. 2011, *Benefits to the private sector of open access to higher education and scholarly research. a research report to JISC from HOST Policy Research*, HOST Policy, Horsham.

Pickover, M & Mohale, G 2013, *Report of the South African Digitisation Initiative (SADI) workshop on digitisation and digital libraries: standards, best practices, policies and technical requirements*, Wits, Library, Johannesburg.

Raju, R & Schoombee, L 2013, 'Research support through the lens of transformation in academic libraries with reference to the case of Stellenbosch University Libraries', South African Journal of Libraries and Information Sciences, vol. 79, no. 2, pp. 27-38.

Raju, R et al 2013, 'Opening access to African scholarly content: Stellenbosch University's AOARI platforms', Insights: the UKSG Journal, vol. 26, no. 1, pp. 44-50.

Raju, R et al. 2012, 'Open access: are we there yet?–the case of Stellenbosch University, South Africa', South African Journal of Libraries and Information Sciences (Special Launch Issue).

Weinberg, BA 2011, 'Developing science: scientific performance and brain drains in the developing world', Journal of Development Economics, vol. 95, no. 1, pp. 95-104.

Willinsky, J 2006, 'Access to power: research in international policymaking', Harvard International Review, no. 2, pp. 54-57.

All websites accessed between May and July 2014.

Conclusion: Roundtable

Pierre Mounier and Joachim Schöpfel

Each chapter of this book tells a story about open access, and each story is different. Obviously, there is no such thing as a unique model of open access. Each country of the BRICS develops its own way to open access. Conditions are too different. Language, culture and history create specific environments of science, economy and law, and each country must face particular challenges and seize its own opportunities. Yet, we can distinguish some common features, above all a strong commitment to open access shared by scientific and political authorities in order to increase the impact of the countries' research output and the availability of scientific information. Science needs communication, and beyond all diversity, new technology and scientific universalism make the development of global approaches possible.

Shared convictions, similar objectives, but unique conditions—concluding the book on open access in emerging countries, we ask our authors to comment on a few questions about open access. We wanted to find out what is common, what is different, what can be learned and what the threats and opportunities for the future development of open access are. They were free to answer or not, and they played the game not only in a personal way but also as ambassadors of their different countries. In the following, we present their answers and comments in the form of a virtual round table so that the reader can make up his own mind on uniqueness, diversity, likeness and connection in the pursuit of open access. The round table was conducted by Pierre Mounier, a historian from the School for Advanced Studies in Social Sciences in Paris[9], and Deputy Director of the French OpenEdition publishing house[10]. His partners were Abel Packer (Brazil), Leonid Pavlov (Russia), Sarika Sawant (India), Dehua Hu (China) and Reggie Raju (South Africa).

Key Factors for Success

The first question was about success. Open access is definitely a success story. What can explain this success? "Which/What are the three key factors for the success of open access?" For Leonid Pavlov, the key factors are of a legal, economic and technological nature. Sarika Sawant shifts the focus to the information market with an increasing number of producers (offer) and consumers (demand) and cheap technology, available to/accessible to everyone. Yet, she adds policy-making as the third critical success factor – because of public policy in favour of open access, government-funded research organisations progress in the adoption of open access strategies at their institutional level.

Regarding the scientific community, Dehua Hu identifies three conditions in support of open access: the return to the nature of scientific research, the reform of the research evaluation system and the redesign of the academic reward system.

According to Reggie Raju: "Research has shown that the research output from Africa is low and one of the primary reasons for this is the poor access to quality research to support findings or hypotheses. Research on African issues is now accessible (with open access) to Africans and has far greater relevance than previously when it was too expensive for the communities that needed it the most – Africans and African researchers. Open access is the impetus for the domino effect for improved output from Africa. The development of improved connectivity, especially on the east coast of Africa, will magnify the success of open access. Another success of open access for Africa is that titles that were small and very local now have the capacity to become international overnight (assuming the quality is of an acceptable standard). The opening up of access to these titles promotes output

---

9   Ecoles des Hautes Etudes en Sciences Sociales (EHESS), http://www.ehess.fr/

10 http://www.openedition.org/

from Africa and facilitates collaboration. There are examples where titles which have become open have resulted in collaboration with researchers from Europe. The growing acceptance that open access is the way of the future, places greater value on the principle of sharing research findings for the benefit of society and mankind. Again, in the African context, it will accelerate the transformation of Africa – South Africa included."

Abel Packer puts it all together: "In many senses, open access is already a success. It has become an inseparable part of the scientific information flow. However, it is facing many political and economic challenges in order to become the predominant way to communicate research. National research policies that favour open access is the main factor to advance open access. The adoption of articles' impact to evaluate research instead of the Impact Factor of the journal where they are published is the second key factor. A third and determinant factor is the emergence of an OA market in place of the subscription model."

Challenges

It is never easy to predict the future. However, we asked what would be the most important challenge for open access in 2015. Dehua Hu and Leonid Pavlov cannot see any particular challenges in their countries in 2015 compared to other years, even if in Russia "the progress of open access will still depend on the improvement of copyright legislation and sufficient funding."

"Filling up the repositories", that is, supporting the growth of the open archives is the major challenge in India. More concerned with journal publishing, Abel Packer identifies the impact of open access journals as a major challenge in 2015 and expects (or hopes for) more open access articles with more impact in the two large academic databases, Web of Sciences and Scopus.

Lack of education, copyright and policy are the major challenges in South Africa: "The greatest challenge is the lack of education about open access and the eradication of the misconception that open access is vanity publishing. Further, the view that content that is 'free' does not necessarily equate to content not having value and not being of the highest scholarly standard, is a fallacy that needs to be eradicated, especially among researchers themselves. The second most significant challenge is that of copyright, including international copyright legislation. The third major challenge from an African perspective is autocratic government that imposes sanctions on content that does not stimulate growth and development" (Reggie Raju).

Sarika Sawant addresses a quite particular problem. For her, another challenge in the near future will be the control of predatory publishers, that is, publishers working with an "exploitative open-access publishing business model that involves charging authors publication fees without providing the editorial and publishing services associated with legitimate journals"[11]. There may be a couple of Indian publishers and journals on Beall's list but this is not a specific Indian challenge.

We also asked if language was a problem for open access. "Inside the debate about open access in your country, is there any connection with the question of multilingualism in scientific publications? If yes, could you explain how?"

Abel Packer: "Multilingualism plays a key role in the communication of research in Latin America. Spanish and Portuguese languages are largely used to communicate research with national focus or interest. Physical and life sciences are mainly communicated in English while social sciences and humanities in the local language". The following replies were given:

Leonid Pavlov: "The language barrier is an important problem in Russia with respect to world-wide open access. Scientific Russian is well developed and has a rich history therefore one can hardly imagine that all Russian scholars will start writing their original works in English. At the same time English is *de facto* a universal language of scientific communication nowadays although many Russian university graduates do not speak English well. The situation is slowly improving as more and more young people are now learning English."

In other words: yes, language is a challenge for open access in emerging countries because of English dominating scientific communication, but not for all countries, and not all disciplines are affected in the same way. Also, as mentioned by Leonid Pavlov, maybe this is a transitory challenge because of the development of English language skills in new generations of scientists.

---

11   Wikipedia contributors, "Predatory open access publishing," *Wikipedia, The Free Encyclopaedia*, http://en.wikipedia.org/w/index.php?title=Predatory_open_access_publishing&oldid=638841197 (accessed December 21, 2014). See also Beall's List of Predatory Publishers at http://scholarlyoa.com/publishers/

Green v Gold Road to Open Access

The open access movement defined "green road" (deposit of documents in open repositories) and "gold road" (article-publishing in open access journals) as the two main approaches to open access publishing of scientific results. Is this distinction of importance for the development of open access in emerging countries?

To the question: "do you think the traditional representation of open access divided between green and gold is relevant to understanding the development of open access in your country?" all authors answered with a "yes it is".

But Leonid Pavlov relativizes; this distinction may be relevant but not really pertinent for the understanding of the development of open access in Russia. And as Reggie Raju states, these "nuances in the difference between green and gold routes are only understood by those who have a deeper understanding of open access. The fundamental principle is that we want scholarly content to be openly accessible to the widest possible audience and the way we get to that point is immaterial to the end user – as long as content is easily available to the end user. What needs to be promoted is the version that is closest to the final one."

Abel Packer (Brazil) draws our attention to the fact that in Brazil, the gold open access road is the model preferred by national institutions.

The Public Sector

Political support appears to be a critical success factor. And as Abel Packer just mentioned, the preferences and choices of national research institutions will shape the development towards open access. Is this sufficient to speak about an alternative model in emerging countries? "BRICS are countries where the public sector plays in important role, particularly for research. Do you think we can see in it an alternative model to the development of a market/private sector-oriented open access in Western countries?"

The answers reveal fundamental differences of experiences and approaches. On the one hand, there is a strong rejection of market models. In the words of Leonid Pavlov: "A market/private sector prays to the only god–money. And as D.H. Lawrence once put it: 'The care about money was like a great cancer, eating away the individuals of all classes'[12]." For Leonid Pavlov, the only sustainable model for the development of research and scientific communication, including open access, is different from market models. Abel Packer seems to share this opinion but objects that "the public sector of developed countries also plays an important role for research and in most of the cases much more than (in) BRICS countries."

According to Sarika Sawant, "in India as far as scientific publications are concerned, they are mostly published by government-funded scientific institutions; hardly any journal takes APC; most of them are available on the Internet and charge negligible amounts for print copy."

The situation is the same in South Africa. Reggie Raju says: "In South Africa, research published via research councils and academic institutions are, for all intents and purposes, funded by the public. Researchers are rewarded for their publication by the national government and it is these rewards that serve as seed money for further research. Essentially, there is already a relationship between the public (via government) and researchers. It is only reasonable to seek a formal relationship that will materialize in an alternate model where all funded research is published (either green or gold) in an open access forum."

On the other hand, Dehua Hu speaking for China states that "the public sector is not an alternative model". Here it clearly appears that open access and the way to organize and develop open access is not only a choice of research communities and scientific policy but it is (also) related to societal developments and economic policies. The gold road option, i.e. open access journal publishing, does not necessarily mean public investment and infrastructures, especially in countries with a significant corporate academic publishing sector and/ or with significant support for private and corporate initiatives. Yet, the green road, that is, open repositories, will always reflect the health and strength of public research and academia.

Cooperation

One characteristic feature of the open access movement is its international, cross-boundary nature. Conferences, networks, forums and blogs are real and virtual spaces for exchanging ideas and learning

---

12 D.H. Lawrence, *Lady Chatterley's lovers*. First edition 1928.

from each other. Is there a specific "BRICS space"? The BRICS countries started to coordinate in crucial fields such as finance, economics, energy and nuclear security. So we wanted to know if "there (is) any discussion, coordination or cooperation between/among BRICS countries regarding the development of open access policies?"

All the authors agree that as far as they know, there is nothing like a coordinated open access policy between/among the BRICS countries up to now. However, there are bilateral initiatives, and Brazil seems to take the lead, as Abel Packer explains: "We are working with South Africa in the development of nationally published journals through SciELO Program that is led by national public research institutions and therefore it is an expression of national open access policies[13]. Last May (2014) we organized the first Brazil-China Bilateral Meeting on STM Publishing"[14]. Reggie Raju confirms: "There has been substantial discussion between the Academy of Sciences of South Africa (ASSAf) and its Brazilian counterparts with regard to open access. The Academy is using the SciELO Platform (a Brazilian platform) for its open access journals". But Abel Packer admits also, that "there is not a systematic forum to discuss scholarly communication and open access".

And what about other countries? "Do the BRICS countries play a leading role towards smaller countries in their regional area regarding open access policies?" Here again, the experiences and policies are different. For China, Dehua Hu cannot see such a leadership in the field of open access because "BRICS countries have a long way to go". Also, even if she endorses the potential role of India for "small countries around like Sri-Lanka or Bangladesh", Sarika Sawant concedes nevertheless that this role is all but evident in this specific sector.

The situation is different in Russia: "Russia does have an influence on the smaller countries mainly on those using the Russian language to communicate with the outer world (e.g. the Central Asian republics) and open access is no exception" (Leonid Pavlov).

The most developed model is Latin America. Here again, SciELO plays a crucial role but the roots are historical. Abel Packer: "In the case of Latin America, there was historically strong cooperation among countries before the emergence of the open access movement.

---

13 http://www.scielo.org.za/

14 http://eventos.scielo.org/brazil-chinameeting/en/program/

SciELO was launched four years before the Budapest Declaration and the development of the SciELO network was led by Brazil and Chile. Brazil is responsible for the maintenance of the SciELO technological platform and plays the role of secretariat of the network but the decisions, process and contents are shared."

On the African continent, South Africa also plays a specific role in the field of open access. According to Reggie Raju, "South Africa is seen as the leader on the continent and must take on this responsibility with action rather than lip-service. Therefore, adoption of OA practices must be infectious to ensure that Africa is a benefactor. South Africa cannot remain an island on the continent and has to assist to ensure that the continent develops holistically (…) The higher education system in South Africa makes provision by supporting countries in the Southern African Development Community (SADC) region. More than contributing to the SADC region, South Africa plays a significant role as a leader on the continent – its research output is the largest of all the other African countries. Given this leadership role, it is hoped that open access practices become common practices among African countries". However, Reggie Raju is not sure that the continent is ready for policy development.

An Alternative Model?

Do the local initiatives and projects of the BRICS countries bear the potential for another way of communicating scientific research? We finally asked the authors of this book if they "see any chance of a global alternative model of open access emerging from the BRICS countries?"

- They answered consistently, in three different ways:

- Today, no, there is no such potential (Dehua Hu). Abel Packer explains why this is so, at least for the Brazilian context: "Because BRICS national research systems value more research that are published in developed countries' journals that present higher impact than nationally published journals. These journals are mainly published by commercial publishers". Another objection is the potential conflict with global models: "South Africa is working on developing a SPARC chapter for open access for Africa. If this proves to be successful, then, is it not possible to develop a chapter for BRICS with one of the key objectives being the development of a global alternative publishing model?" (Reggie Raju). In other

words, there may (will) be alternative models but they are global and not specifically BRICS models.
- Maybe in the future. Sarika Sawant as well as Dehua Hu do not exclude the possibility that in the future, the development of open access will produce a different, alternative model of scientific communication. Yet, it remains unclear today how and why.
- Yes, the potential is there but it depends on specific conditions. We can distinguish two levels. First, the emergence of an alternative requests a favourable political environment: "It depends on the general success of the BRICS project and the Russians sincerely support this newly emerging union" (Leonid Pavlov). Second, such an alternative should rely on successful projects, such as SciELO: "The SciELO Model represents an open access solution that could be adopted by developed countries to publish their journals that are not under commercial publishers" (Abel Packer).

Learning from the BRICS

The debate is open. Michael Jubb stated in the preface to this book that "the challenges to be met in the transition to open access are as powerful in the BRICS as they are in the global North. Meeting and overcoming them requires concerted and determined action from governments, funding organisations, universities and, not least, researchers themselves". Our round table confirms this need for political support, scientific engagement and coordination in favour of open access. It confirms too, the impact of local conditions and the crucial importance for projects and initiatives to meet these challenges and to adapt global models to local constraints.

Brazil, Russia, India, China and South Africa all developed their own way to open access, based on specific blends of green and gold road, public investment and private initiatives. What they have in common, is their commitment to research as a driver of economic and societal development and to open science as a way to enhance quality, impact and access to scientific information. Open access is not an end in itself but a means to better science.

Perhaps there is no unique or dominant model of open access. Perhaps there never will be. Perhaps, too, there is no need for a unique model, be it green or gold. Diversity may be a better option for sustainable development. However, based on the experience of the

BRICS countries and our debate we can say that even if every country has to determine its own special way to open access, they can learn from each other, and they are already doing so. Learning from each other does not only mean learning from failures, mistakes and dead-ends but more so and above all, learning from success.

More than the understanding of problems and challenges, perhaps the real message of our book is the importance of success stories. The development of open access depends on the promotion of successful initiatives, such as SciELO in Latin America. Expect success, focus on it, and coordinate scientific and political efforts in favour of open science. The future will show how the international research community will realize and transform the tremendous potential of open access and open science. The future is open. But the BRICS countries will be a central part of it.

Further reading

Bartling, S & Friesike, S 2014, *Opening science*, Springer, Heidelberg.

Burns, CS 2014, 'Academic libraries and open access strategies', in *Advances in library administration and organization*, eds. DE Williams & J Golden, Emerald, Bingley, pp. 147-211.

Harnad, S et al. 2004, 'The access/impact problem and the green and gold roads to open access.', *Serials Review*, vol. 30, no. 4, pp. 310-314.

Hodgson, C 2014, 'Open access infrastructure: where we are and where we need to go', *Information Standards Quarterly*, vol. 26, no. 2, pp. 4-14

Lynch, CA 2003, *Institutional repositories: essential infrastructure for scholarship in the digital age*, ARL, Association of Research Libraries, Washington.

Suber, P 2012, *Open access*, The MIT Press, Cambridge.

Vincent, N & Wickham, C 2013, *Debating open access*, British Academy for the Humanities and Social Sciences, London.

Weinberg, BA 2011, 'Developing science: scientific performance and brain drains in the developing world', *Journal of Development Economics*, vol. 95, no. 1, pp. 95-104.

Willinsky, J 2005, *The access principle*, The MIT Press, Cambridge.

Xia, J 2012, 'Diffusionism and open access', *Journal of Documentation*, vol. 68, no. 1, pp. 72-99.

About the Author

Pierre Mounier is deputy director of OpenEdition, a comprehensive infrastructure based in France for open access publication and communication in the humanities and social sciences. OpenEdition offers several platforms for journals, scientific announcements, academic blogs, and, finally, books, in different languages and from different countries. Pierre teaches digital humanities at the EHESS in Paris. He has published several books about the social and political impact of ICT (Les Maîtres du Réseau, les enjeux politiques d'Internet 2001), digital publishing (L'Edition électronique, with Marin Dacos, 2010) and digital humanities (Read/Write Book 2, Une introduction aux humanités numériques, 2012). As deputy director of OpenEdition, Pierre Mounier's work mainly revolves around the development of an internationalisation strategy for the infrastructure, in particular by establishing partnerships with platforms and institutions in Europe and elsewhere . To further this objective, he regularly participates in international conferences and seminars to present OpenEdition's programmes and discuss subjects relating to digital humanities and open access. Pierre Mounier participates in the activities of Dariah, the European infrastructure for digital humanities, and co-pilots the "Open Access" group within the French infrastructure BSN.

Web Resources

Declarations

BUDAPEST
http://www.budapestopenaccessinitiative.org/read

BERLIN
http://openaccess.mpg.de/Berlin-Declaration

BETHESDA
http://legacy.earlham.edu/~peters/fos/bethesda.htm

SALVADOR
http://www.icml9.org/public/documents/pdf/en/Dcl-Salvador-OpenAccess-en.pdf

SAN FRANCISCO DECLARATION ON RESEARCH ASSESSMENT
http://am.ascb.org/dora/

LYON DECLARATION ON ACCESS TO INFORMATION AND DEVELOPMENT (IFLA)
http://www.lyondeclaration.org/

Directories

COMMUNITY: OPEN ACCESS DIRECTORY (OAD)
http://oad.simmons.edu/oadwiki/Main_Page

COMMUNITY: OPEN ACCESS SCHOLARLY INFORMATION SOURCEBOOK (OASIS)
http://www.openoasis.org/

INSTITUTIONS: THE COALITION OF OPEN ACCESS POLICY INSTITUTIONS (COAPI)
http://www.sparc.arl.org/COAPI

JOURNALS: DIRECTORY OF OPEN ACCESS JOURNALS (DOAJ)
http://doaj.org/

REPOSITORIES: DIRECTORY OF OPEN ACCESS REPOSITORIES (OpenDOAR)
http://www.opendoar.org/

REPOSITORIES: REGISTER OF OPEN ACCESS REPOSITORIES (ROAR)
http://roar.eprints.org/

REPOSITORIES: CONFEDERATION OF OPEN ACCESS REPOSITORIES (COAR)
https://www.coar-repositories.org/

News, blogs, other sites

ARCHIVING POLICIES: REGISTRY OF OPEN ACCESS REPOSITORIES MANDATORY ARCHIVING POLICIES (ROARMAP)
http://roarmap.eprints.org/

PUBLISHER COPYRIGHT POLICIES AND SELF-ARCHIVING (SHERPA/RoMEO)
http://www.sherpa.ac.uk/romeo/

CREATIVE COMMONS LICENSES
http://creativecommons.org/licenses/?lang=en

SEARCH ENGINE: BIELEFELD ACADEMIC SEARCH ENGINE (BASE)
http://www.base-search.net/

NEWS: JISC OPEN ACCESS
http://www.jisc.ac.uk/open-access

NEWS: PETER SUBER'S BLOG
https://plus.google.com/u/0/+PeterSuber/posts

NEWS: HEATHER MORRISON'S BLOG
http://poeticeconomics.blogspot.fr

NEWS: STEVAN HARNAD'S BLOG
http://openaccess.eprints.org

NEWS: LIBGUIDE TO OPEN ACCESS
http://libguides.wits.ac.za/openaccess_a2k_scholarly_communication

NEWS: OPEN ACCESS AND SCIENTIFIC INFORMATION (FRENCH)
http://openaccess.inist.fr/

EVENTS: OPEN ACCESS WEEK
http://www.openaccessweek.org/

Protocol: The Open Archives Initiative Protocol for Metadata Harvesting
   http://www.openarchives.org/OAI/openarchivesprotocol.html

Bibliography on Open Access by Charles W. Bailey
   http://www.digital-scholarship.org/tsp/transforming.htm

Index

academies of science
    Academy of Science of South Africa, 175, 197
    Chinese Academy of Sciences, 137, 140
    Indian Academy of Sciences, 99-100, 105-6, 111
    Russian Academy of Sciences, 75-79

All-Russian Institute for Scientific and Technical Information (VINITI), 70

archiving. *See* institutional repositories

article processing charges (APC), 3, 10, 53, 132, 183-85

arXiv, 9, 63, 69

Berlin Declaration, 2, 11, 77, 129

Bethesda Declaration, 2, 11

bibliometrics, 41-43, 169-70
    Journal Citation Reports, 38, 41-42, 111, 130-32

BIREME
    bibliographic control and, 41
    CNPq partnership with, 39
    international technical cooperation, 30
    role in Latin America for IT development, 32-34, 36
    MEDLINE database and, 33-34, 43
    SciELO development and, 36-39
    Virtual Health Library (VHL), 32, 34-36, 38-39, 44

brain drain, 167-69

Budapest Declaration, 2, 8-9, 11, 28, 129

Budapest Open Access Initiative (BOAJ), 129

Centre for Information Technologies and Systems, Russia (CITIS), 71-75, 84-86

China Association for Science and Technology (CAST), 130-31

China National Knowledge Infrastructure (CNKI) full-text databases, 132-34

Chinese Academy of Sciences (CAS), 137, 140

Chinese development of OA, 129-32, 135-38, 147-49
    regional inequalities, 144-45

citation
    as access indicator, 11, 38, 41-44, 47, 56-57, 86, 169-70, 182
    Chinese S&T Journal Citation Report, 130-32
    Russian Science Citation Index, 76, 79

CITIS. *See* Centre for Information Technologies and Systems

CNPq, 36-37, 39, 45

copyright law
    access restrictions and, 166, 177-79, 193
    China and, 130, 149
    Indian initiatives and, 112-13
    libraries and, 180
    public vs. publishers' interest, 64
    Russian, 69, 82-87
    South African, 181-82

Council of Scientific and Industrial Research, India (CSIR), 93, 99, 101, 110, 114

Creative Commons, 69, 85-87

Declaration of San José, 34

democracy and OA, 161-64

depository law. *See also* institutional repositories
Russian, 72-73, 80

digital revolution, 8

Directory of Open Access Books (DOAB), 112

Directory of Open Access Journals (DOAJ), 27, 82
China, 125, 129-30, 138
India, 104-5, 108
language barrier and, 145
social responsibility and, 82-83

Directory of Open Access Repositories (OpenDOAR), 9-10
India, 99
Russia, 63, 69
South Africa, 177-78

DOAJ. *See* Directory of Open Access Journals

educational resources
Indian, 110-12
Russian, 79-82
SciELO, 51

electronic publishing
archival access, 141-42, 146
Brazilian. *See* SciELO
Chinese scientific, 126, 138-40
online submission systems, 141
promotion in India, 110-11
Russian, 70-78

FAPESP. *See* São Paulo Research Foundation

funding of OA resources, 2-5, 163-64, 168
business model of, 87
challenges, 193-94
governmental, 67-69, 87
institutional, 183
SciELO, 36-40

gold road, 10-11, 86, 104, 199
green vs., 195-96

Google. *See also* search engines
Analytics, 52
Scholar, 43, 51, 164

government support for OA, 195-96
Russia, 67-69, 87
South Africa, 174-76

green road, 9, 11, 86, 93-94, 104, 196
gold vs., 195-96

GSNTI. *See* State System for Scientific and Technical Information

high-impact publishing, 40-41, 49-51, 106-8, 148, 170-71, 198
See also quality control

Indian Council of Agricultural Research (ICAR), 93

Indian Institute of Science (IISc), 93, 98, 100-101

Indian Institutes of Technology (IIT), 93, 99-100, 106

Institute of Scientific Information (ISI), 38, 42

institutional repositories. *See also* depository law
India, 99-104, 113-16
Indian Institute of Science, 98
librarians and, 176-77, 180
policy in Russia, 80-82
policy in South Africa, 181-83

promotion of, 113, 166-67
South African development of, 159-60, 165-66, 177-80

intellectual property rights
differences between Russia and Western countries, 68-69
legal aspects, 64, 83-86
protecting authors', 149, 175

international cooperation, 29-30
arXiv, 9, 63, 69
SciELO, 197-98

Journal Citation Reports (JCR)
Chinese S&T, 130-32
SciELO development and, 38

language barrier, 53-55, 69-70, 137-38, 145, 194
Directory of Open Access Journals and, 145

Latin American and caribbean Center on Health Statistics. *See* BIREME

Latin American and Caribbean Health Sciences Literature (LILACS) database, 33-34, 41

Latindex, 37, 46

MEDLINE database, 33-34, 43

Ministry of Science and Education (Russia), 79-82
See also Russian Academy of Sciences

National Council for Scientific and Technological Development (CNPq), 36-37, 39, 45

OpenDOAJ. *See* Directory of Open Access Journals

OpenDOAR. *See* Directory of Open Access Repositories

OpenEdition publishing house, 16m 125, 192, 202

Pan-American Health Organization (PAHO). *See under* World Health Organization

peer review
credibility and, 71, 107-10
publication requirements, 76-79, 85, 175
SciELO and, 52-54

philosophy of OA, 155-56, 160-61

predatory publishing, 93, 108-10, 194

public sector support for OA. *See* government support for OA

quality control, 36-38, 85-86, 148
See also high-impact publishing
See also peer review

Register of Open Access Repositories (ROAR), 77, 99, 101-2, 115

research collaboration, 13-14, 31-32, 167-69

Russian Academy of Sciences (RAS). *See also* Ministry of Science and Education
Central Economics and Mathematics Institute (CEMI) institutional repository, 77-78
e-Library, 75-76
Siberian Section, 78-79
Social Sciences department, 76-78

Salvador Declaration on Open Access, 45, 55

São Paulo Research Foundation (FAPESP), 36-39, 41, 45

SciELO
bibliographic control and bibliometrics, 41-43
bilateral international initiatives, 197-98
Brazil Collection, 47-49

Financial and administrative management, 38-40
goal of, 40
international impact, 49-50
South Africa (SciELO-SA), 174-76
Thomson Reuters and, 43-44

Scopus
challenges of OA, 193
India's OA movement and, 107, 114
SciELO's international impact and, 14, 49

search engines, 10, 80, 101, 133, 164, 167
See also Google

serials crisis, 10-11

Socionet system (Russia), 76-78

South African development of OA, 164, 167-68

Soviet Union and OA, 63, 67-69

State System for Scientific and Technical Information (Russia), 67-68

UNESCO
CDS/ISIS software package, 30-31, 82
cooperative information networks, 32
funding for OA initiatives, 97
Information for All Program (IFAP), 29

United States National Library of Medicine (NLM), 31-33

Universities of Technology, South Africa (UoT), 164-65, 179, 181

VINITI. *See* All-Russian Institute for Scientific and Technical Information

Virtual Health Library (VHL), 32, 34-36, 38-39, 44

visibility
OA's effect on, 183-85
paradox of OA, 170-71
SciELO and, 36-38, 40-41

VNTIC. *See* Centre for Information Technologies and Systems

Web of Science (WoS)
challenges of OA, 193
Core Collection, 27
SciELO as an alternative to, 43
SciELO Citation Index as part of, 44

World Health Organization (WHO)
cooperative information networks, 32
Pan-American Health Organization (PAHO), 30, 33, 39, 44

209

About the Author

Hélène Prost is information professional at the Institute of Scientific and Technical Information (CNRS) and associate member of the GERiiCO research laboratory (University of Lille 3). She is interested in empirical library and information sciences and statistical data analysis. She participates in research projects on evaluation of collections, document delivery, usage analysis, grey literature and open access, and she is author of several publications.

www.ingramcontent.com/pod-product-compliance
Lightning Source LLC
Chambersburg PA
CBHW051357290426
44108CB00015B/2050